WHAT IS SOUL?

by DAVID BLOOM

Copyright © 2019 by David Bloom

All rights reserved. No part of this book may be reproduced or used in any manner without written permission of the copyright owner except for the use of quotations in a book review.

First paperback edition March 2019
Edited by Barbara Kaplan
Book cover design by Reynaldo Certain

ISBN 978-0-9769148-4-6

Fire & Form Publishing
226 S. Wabash #700
Chicago Il. 60604

www.WhatIsSoul.com

TABLE OF CONTENTS

A Word from the Author	7
Interviewees	9
Editor's Note	17
Soul in a Few Words	21
Soul and Religion	27
Soul and You	43
Individuality: The Essence of Being Human	47
The Birth of a Soul	55
The Growth of a Soul	59
Soul Sources	71
The Soul and Death	81
Soul Expressions	85
Soul in Music	89
Jazz	93
Soul Music of the 1950s and '60s	97
Soul Brothers	101

Soul or Not?	105
Soulful Music Around the World	111
Coltrane and The Avant Garde	115
New Generations	119
Soul Without Notes	123
Soul to Soul	139
Soul on Earth	161
The Soul of Nations	165
High-Tech Soul	179
The Speed of Soul	185
Soulless	191
Soul Repair	207
Holding on to Your Soul	227
Afterword	236
Acknowledgements	238

A WORD FROM THE AUTHOR

The first time I heard the word soul, I was a kid in the sixties. Whether it was James Brown, The Temptations, Muddy Waters or my teacher, Buddy Guy, "soul" was a popular term to describe music played by black musicians. To me, this music expressed distinct human emotions without any facade.

Listening to soulful music, I didn't feel like I was being conned or sold something I didn't want. I was witnessing music that demonstrated deep humanity while revealing a full spectrum of feelings. The authenticity was palpable and, as a result, the effect on me was dramatic. I pretty much eliminated listening to most white purveyors of popular hits. I hadn't figured out where soul would fit in my life, and I didn't yet know that I would focus the rest of my days on a search for truth, authenticity, and passion: the elements of what I consider to be soul.

I started seeing soul all around me. Even before my introduction to black music, I remember going to Rodfei Zedek Synagogue in Chicago's Hyde Park, where I listened to Rabbi Ralph Simon's Saturday morning sermons, filled with wisdom, but more importantly, with what I would later realize was soul on steroids. What he communicated far surpassed the religion with its obligatory liturgy and spoke right to my heart. It seemed to me most members of the congregation didn't believe in the rituals; they just wanted to maintain an attachment to the community. I felt no connection to the religion, other than the great reverence I had for the traditions of some Jewish writers, musicians, directors, rabbis and thinkers, who had qualities I now define as soulful. All of these geniuses transcended religion, as any original thinker must.

Because of what I have experienced with thousands of people, one of my main objectives in writing this book was to uncouple the word "soul" from its ties to blackness and religion. There are too many contexts for soul and soulfulness to be limited only by these two. Soul can be found anywhere and everywhere, not just in Jewish or African-American culture.

Soul permeates music, drama and art - even business and law. Soul seasons our food; we savor our "soul food," whatever its ethnic origin. Soul, of course, has religious connotations: the concept of The Soul. Do we exist before birth and after death? Are there spirits? Every individual has a soul. Souls interact when people get together, either one-on-one or in groups, communities or nations. In America, soul occupies a unique place, whether through its existence or nonexistence. But soul has its costs and can easily be lost. Soul can be found and developed, and its manifestations can change the world.

For the last forty-five years, teaching jazz improvisation to thousands of students, I have been doing my best to help people reveal their souls in what many believe is the language of the soul: music. Because it often lacks explicit words, music has to rely on its ability to communicate a more abstract, emotional message. That became clear to me growing up in the '60s, discovering black music where there was a larger commitment to expression, to living and not just surviving, that was absent elsewhere. For me, jazz was a holistic activity, involving heart, head and hands: emotions, intellect and body.

During the past fifteen years, I interviewed people from as many demographics as possible: most races and ages, from children to the elderly, chefs to CEOs, religious to secular, young students to PhDs, political to apolitical, unknown to celebrated. They provided a plethora of definitions, attitudes and life experiences. Some defined soul explicitly, others implicitly – through their stories.

My goal is for you to be stimulated by the stories and definitions and begin to appreciate the breadth of soul and soulfulness in yourself and others. I hope reading this book will elevate your life.

David Bloom

INTERVIEWEES

OSCAR BROWN, JR. was, according to the Los Angeles Times, the most hyphenated figure in show business: poet/singer/songwriter/actor/playwright/producer/director-lyricist/humanitarian. In addition to writing and producing (both on and off Broadway) such shows **Big Time Buck White** and **Kicks & Company**, Brown composed lyrics to the hit songs "Dat Dere," "The Snake" and "Work Song," among many others. He also hosted radio and television programs, including several on PBS.

TOM BURRELL was CEO of Burrell Communications, one of the largest multicultural marketing firms in the world. After coining the phrase "Black people are not dark-skinned white people," Burrell acquired accounts for Coca-Cola, McDonald's, Procter and Gamble, American Airlines, Allstate and Toyota, to name just a few. Winner of countless awards, Burrell is now retired and developing his talent as a musician.

WENDY CLINARD performs and teaches flamenco dance and heads the dance company, Clinard Dance.

TED COHEN was chair of the department of philosophy at the University of Chicago. Author of a book on the philosophy of humor, *Jokes: Philosophical Thoughts on Joking Matters*, he was famous for finding the extraordinary in the ordinary.

CLIFF COLNOT is a composer, arranger, producer and conductor in both classical music and jazz. For many years he conducted the Civic Orchestra of Chicago as well as the Chicago Symphony Orchestra's Contemporary MusicNOW ensemble. He is currently a faculty member of the DePaul University School of Music.

ANDREA COSNOWSKY, formerly a Nashville songwriter, now serves Congregation Etz Chaim in DuPage County, Illinois, as Senior Rabbi.

BARRETT DOSS, at the time of her interview, was an eighth-grade student at the University of Chicago Lab School. As an adult she is a film and theatre actor known for her role as Rita Hanson in the Broadway production of *Groundhog Day* and as the character Victoria Hughes on the TV series *Station 19*.

Fellow eighth grade students interviewed for this book were:

TOM BREWER

DEREK CHIAMPAS

CHRISSY DELACOTTA

ZACK GRAHAM

NATHAN WORCESTER

ANN SAWYER

CHRISTIAN STEINBARTH

JON SWANK

PHILLIP VERNA

VAN SANDWICK

ERWIN DRECHSLER is a chef and former owner of the eponymous restaurant, Erwin.

BILL HORBERG is a Hollywood film producer known for such films as *Cold Mountain*, *The Talented Mr. Ripley*, and *Searching for Bobby Fischer*, among others. He is married to artist Elsa Mora.

CHARLES JAFFE is a psychiatrist in Chicago, practicing for over twenty years at the Rush University Medical Center.

RICK KOGAN is a journalist and radio/television host in Chicago. He has authored eight books about people and institutions in his home town, including one about the famous Billy Goat Tavern.

BILL KURTIS is a television journalist, narrator, documentary producer and news anchor with a thirty-year career at CBS. He also wrote the books *On Assignment*, *Death Penalty on Trial*, and *Prairie Table Cookbook*. His credits as a narrator and documentarian are too numerous for even one page.

DAVE LIEBMAN is a world-famous saxophonist and flutist. In 2010 the National Endowment for the Arts gave him a Jazz Masters lifetime achievement award. Currently, he teaches at the Manhattan School of Music and offers clinics and master classes at schools around the globe.

BLANCHE MANNING is a law professor and federal judge in Chicago. She is also known as a talented jazz saxophone instrumentalist.

DON MEADE, known as The Jazz Griot, entertained and educated future generations by sharing his unique stories and intimate knowledge of the giants of jazz. The Donald Meade Legacy Society, in conjunction with the African American Jazz Caucus, has established an award in his name.

ELSA MORA is a visual artist. Originally from Cuba, she now lives in the United States where she is married to film producer Bill Horberg, also featured in this book. Her artwork, in a variety of mediums, depicts universal issues of identity, connectivity, and survival.

NATALIJA NOGULICH is an actress and author with hundreds of film and television credits. She portrayed Josephine Hoffa in the film **Hoffa** and is best known for her performances as Vice Admiral Alynna Nechayev on several iterations of the **Star Trek** series. She also teaches at the American Film Institute and other universities and wrote the historical novel, **One Woman's War**.

JEWEL TANCY is a singer-songwriter based in Chicago. Composer of hundreds of tunes, she was featured on Chicago's PBS station, WTTW, in the concert film, **Cool Heat**.

STUDS TERKEL was an author, broadcaster, actor and historian, known for his many books of interviews including **Hard Times** and **Working**, which became a Broadway show. He was one of Chicago's cultural icons, with a show that ran for generations on the radio station WFMT, famous for its arts and classical music programming.

PATTI VASQUEZ, aka Lipstick Mom, is an internationally known standup comedian as well as a radio and television personality. She currently hosts the show *Pretty Late with Patti Vasquez* on the AM radio station WGN. In addition, she founded an organization called With Kind Words that provides healthcare consultation and promotes compassionate communication practices.

BOB WILLEMS works as a consultant for non-profit organizations, developing fundraising campaigns, websites, and strategic online planning.

YOU, the reader. Your personal experiences, views and biases will play into how you read and interpret the stories and thoughts of others. Read with an open mind as this is a chance to explore your own soul as well.

EDITOR'S NOTE

Before I started editing this book, the raw transcripts inspired me to search out my own soul and see how I could make necessary improvements. David Bloom selected thirty-one soulful individuals to interview; even the children seemed particularly wise. However, because these interviews stretched over a fifteen-year period, some of the references may appear to be dated, and some of the participants have died. Not that that matters. The issue is truth, and truth ought to be eternal.

This book is structured in what I regard as a logical sequence, although other arrangements could have worked. First, a few short attempts at defining soul function as a prelude. Then, because the original context for the word "soul" belongs to the domain of religion, comes a chapter on The Soul, followed by one on the (small letter) souls of individual people. The next chapter concerns itself with how these individuals express their souls in various vocations and avocations.

Moving outward, the following chapter considers various ways in which souls interact, and the chapter after that discusses the souls of communities, ethnic groups, and nations as a whole. Since souls run the risk of deterioration and loss, a chapter on the cost of soul appears next, followed by a discussion on how damaged souls can be repaired, and finally, various methods to maintain them.

It is not necessary to read each chapter in successive order. You as a reader might want to consider some of the material slowly – and pause a bit while doing so.

Barbara Kaplan

SOUL:

1: the immaterial essence, animating principle or actuating cause of an individual life.

2: the spiritual principle embodied in human beings, all rational and spiritual beings, or the universe.

3: a person's total self.

4: an active or essential part; a moving spirit.

5: the moral and emotional nature of human beings; the quality that arouses emotion and sentiment; spiritual or moral force.

6: person, personification.

7: a strong positive feeling (as of intense sensitivity and emotional fervor) conveyed especially by African American performers; cultural consciousness and pride among people of African heritage.

-Merriam-Webster.com

SOUL IN A FEW WORDS

ELSA MORA: Soul, what is soul? Well, in Spanish it's alma. Alma, that's a beautiful word, so let's say it's the accumulation of human experience expressed through the individuality of every person.

JEWEL TANCY: My definition of 'soul' is pretty big. I think soul is the force that's inside of all of us, the force that makes me breathe, the force that makes me feel, express. It makes me touch things; it makes me happy, sad. Soul makes me accountable. Soul is very personal. But it's something that we all share.

WENDY CLINARD: Soul is a cool word, right? We use it out of context a lot. But soul is so many things. I think that one of the more important parts of soul is an absolute openness. It is openness and complete abandonment of apology. There's no litigating for things, it's like boom! This is what I got in this very moment.

RICK KOGAN: You can define soul in many ways as knowing (and this may be the hardest thing) what's real in yourself and the willingness to display it in a genuine fashion. It still amazes me that people think, "Well, we all have soul, and we can cash it in like a lottery ticket when we're dead, to get to some place we don't even know exists," instead of experiencing it right here, where I think it should be experienced. If it exists at all!

DAVE LIEBMAN: In a way, we are talking about something that we can't locate, we can't describe. We can't say it's three millimeters, it's gray, it's a mass, it's a muscle, it's bone, it looks like a glob or it looks like a flower. We don't even know what the heck it is. One thing is for sure: You got it! If you see it, you recognize it.

RICK KOGAN: I'm not thinking of soul all the time. I don't like to use that word, because it's misused so often. It's kind of like the way people think about art: "I don't really know what art is, but I know it when I see it." Well, that's bullshit!

ERWIN DRECHSLER: I think that it's extremely important to be aware of the concept of soul and spirit. It's something that we can neglect, we can lose focus on. It's believing. It's faith. It's sharing, it's love.

ZACK GRAHAM: Soul is a combination of will. It's a combination of faith. It's a combination of knowing yourself. It's a combination of truth. It's a force, it's very powerful, and it exists in every one of us.

BLANCHE MANNING: Soul is like spiritual empowerment. It's something that brings out the humanity in people. It makes people who have soul understand that other people are human, and they're entitled to consideration for whatever the situation might be.

ANNE SAWYER: Soul is the thing that enables everyone to feel emotion. I think you're born with it, and you can change it. It's not just a given thing.

ZACK GRAHAM: Soul is something that can either be nurtured and cared for and looked after, or it can be put on the back burner, put in the closet, and you can do whatever you need to do.

ELSA MORA: Soul is not in stone or in objects. To me it's a place where I feel very comfortable. It's something that I've been building over years and years and years. I think that's the way soul is born into every person. It takes a long time.

DON MEADE: That soul thing – it's about truth. It's all we have, it's the marrow of our bones, it's the ultimate of us. Here I am! What you see is what you get. That's it.

TED COHEN: Everybody has soul. It's like that old spiritual, right? "Rockin' My Soul in the Bosom of Abraham." Everybody has his soul rocked in the bosom of Abraham. But there's another sense of the word in which it means the capacity for deep and almost immediate expression of feeling.

DON MEADE: Soul is charisma. It goes with you. Some people are charismatic, others are not. Those who have charisma continue to spread the message. They are messengers; their mere presence is a magnetic force that demands attention, and they get that attention by virtue of what they're saying.

PATTI VASQUEZ: Soulfulness is having something to say. It's what speaks to you, the way you express yourself. It's not just being a body. It's what drives you in the world.

STUDS TERKEL: Soul is something separated from the body, from the corporeal being. But in my case, I don't separate the two; it's one. It's either there or it's not. I don't think you can pin down soul: "This is it." I think each person interprets it in his or her own way.

ZACK GRAHAM: Soul is something that comes out in the stuff you love to do. It comes out whether you love to play music, you love to do sports, you love to make money. That's where soul really shines.

CHARLES JAFFE: Soul comes out through the stories people tell. In the right kind of atmosphere, it's very humbling the way people can really express the things that are so central to their motivations, their fears, their hopes, their dreads, their highest level of aspirations, and their most shame-filled kinds of dark-side moments. I think that, taken together, that's what feels like soul and soulful, and it's uniquely human.

ANDREA COSNOWSKY: I believe soul is that we are all parts of God, little vessels, if you will. I think we have a choice at different parts of our lives when we can feel that still small voice inside of us that it talks about in the Bible. Listen to that voice. That voice is really our soul speaking to us.

TED COHEN: If you want to talk more about soul, you should go to divinity school.

SOUL AND RELIGION

Therevada Buddhism novices truthseeker08

The soul is not a physical entity, but instead refers to everything about us that is not physical – our values, memories, identity, sense of humor. Since the soul represents the parts of the human being that are not physical, it cannot get sick, it cannot die, it cannot disappear. In short, the soul is immortal.

-Harold Kushner

In Biblical times and in ancient Greece, the word "soul" referred to The Soul, that eternal essence of a person that is said to persist before birth and after death. This concept belongs in the realm of theology. Religions often provide people with the means to express their soulfulness; they offer believers a feeling of hope. Souls can be saved – but they also can be sold to the Devil.

In this chapter, people talk about death and how they wonder – particularly as children – whether a soul is snuffed out or continues after its body expires. They discuss the meaning of life; their experiences in church, synagogue, or nature; their visions of God or their inability to conceive of a divine being at all. Ultimately, they question whether a soulful religion can have any impact on their temporal behavior.

DAVID BLOOM: In most people's minds the context for soul is religion. When did you first think of soul or The Soul?

BILL HORBERG: I remember it vividly as a public school student at the Nettelhorst School on Broadway in Chicago. I was in fourth grade or fifth grade. There was a lot of gang activity, gang fights, gang warfare. There was a kid from my sister's school that got beaten to death with a baseball bat in the schoolyard, a boy named Hipolito Vega. The name I can still remember, forty years later, even though I probably only saw him maybe once or twice. But I remember the disruption on the community and the deep tragic sense that hung over us really young, formative kids.

The funeral service for this young boy who was killed, and the sense of his soul being snuffed up, that was probably the first time something registered with me deeply in terms of what is in the skin and in the shell of our bodies. What's really the spirit and the spark that's contained within? Having seen it snuffed out in such a vivid way probably formed some deep impression in my mind.

ANDREA COSNOWSKY: I went to my father when I was five, and I asked him about God. I said, "What happens when we die?" My father gave the party line which was "When you're dead, you're dead." I found that to be a very frightening concept as a five-year-old. I wish on some level my dad might have maybe lied to me a little bit, and it sent me on my own spiritual quest which was: Could that be all there is? When we're gone from this life, that's it?

RICK KOGAN: I'm not a big believer in moving on after this life. This is it, this is it for me and I've got to make it the best, most interesting trip. You know, I am who I am, through genetics, DNA, and the environment. That's it! It's the rarest thing imaginable that I'm not a tiger or a ladybug. That I can function, and enjoy things, and taste things, and drink things and do things. And I'm not in a cage. And my lifespan should be many decades. I don't want to die thinking that I didn't take advantage of my one shot.

STUDS TERKEL: Soul's often associated with theology and religion, as it should be. Jerry Falwell has one impression of soul. The Archbishop of Canterbury has a wholly different impression of soul. I'm sure that a gay bishop has one impression of soul and someone like Pat Robertson a wholly different impression of soul. Whatever that is, it's what makes each of us unique, no matter how successful we might be, or whatever work we do. The word soul is so broad and all-encompassing in its interpretation, you can go any way you want with it, see. Basically, I would say something that has a depth of feeling to it.

Tom Paine, the visionary of the American Revolution, the most eloquent visionary, spoke of some kind of deity – a deist, he called himself. He didn't believe in an anthropomorphic god, but he was not an atheist or an agnostic, he was a deist because he believed in some sort of life force that could be called godlike. I suppose you'd say, in that sense, there's a god in each person. You want to say soul is God, too. One word, one term equals the other. And how God works his wonders to perform or blunders to perform, it's within that person.

CHRISSY DELACOTTA: I think that you're born with a soul that's eternal and even though your body's gone, your soul lives on, and it goes to Heaven or Hell, depending on how your life turns out or what decisions you make. You can make decisions that don't have to do with your soul. Someone can be soulful without being religious. I think they're two different entities, but they cross paths constantly.

DON MEADE: Religion and soulfulness… Well, it depends on what you believe, okay? If you believe religiously, then everything you have comes out. Time is the same way. There's only one thing you can do with time: that's spend it. It's how you spend it. And this is all about that soul. Knowing the component parts, what you can do, what's available to you in this celestial environment of yours, because we all come here alone and we'll leave the same way. Soul is life. It *is* life. The only game we don't know is "Where does it go when life no longer exists?" Maybe someday we'll find out.

RICK KOGAN: It's funny, but when everybody dies, even if they have a million bucks, twenty million bucks, the thing they want (I would hazard to say, most of all) is to think that they have a soul, because that means they're going to move on. That means that life is not over.

DAVID BLOOM: "I'm a believer…"

RICK KOGAN: Right, "I'm a believer, oh yeah, I believe, but I've never said hello to anybody. I hate black people. I hate Jews. I hate Asians. I hate people of color. But, if I die, my soul will take me right up there."

DAVID BLOOM: "Because I go to church every Sunday."

RICK KOGAN: Hypocrites! Well, they don't go to church every Sunday! The people who are religious and talk soul all the time, "Oh, I have a soul," are the people who have that soul lottery ticket stuck in their wallet. If there is such a thing as soul, why wouldn't you exercise it while you're alive? Man, it's not like some annuity you get to cash in the day you die, after fucking people over your whole life.

PHILLIP VERNA: If everyone has a soul then we can become more religious. Religion is a place where people go to express their soul. If they are deeply religious, let's say they are really Orthodox Jews or something like that, then maybe the synagogue is a place for them to express their soul.

ZACK GRAHAM: I'm not any religion, I'm really not. But what I believe is that people use religion as a device. People use religion to find their soul. People use religion to find who they are and what they're about. They can do that through the wisdoms the Bible brings out in people. The Bible brings a lot of stuff out in people, and it's a great tool. (I'm not saying it's not holy or anything.) It's a great tool that people use to find their religion even if they don't realize it.

Faith is the daring of the soul to go farther than it can see.
-William Newton Clarke

CHRISSY DELACOTTA: It's been hard for me to figure out my religion and how I feel about religion, because the more people I meet and the more people I talk to, I have to think about it more and more. When you're young, you're just told what to think, and you're like okay, Jesus is the Son of God. Whatever. As you talk to more and more people, you start to think well, maybe that's not true. You start to question. I think that religion – just having it in my life as a young person – has impacted my soul, because I think it gives you something to believe in. When you have something to believe in, you search for answers. You search for questions. You want to live out your life to the best of your abilities, because you feel there's something on the other side. That your life isn't meaningless.

JON SWANK: Religion was basically created because a lot of people just lacked hope. And then we probably would have ended thousands of years ago because religion makes people continue to go. Maybe for some people, their soul gives them hope instead of their religion, or maybe it is both. I think they are kind of connected there.

ZACK GRAHAM: Some criminals, they completely convert and start worshiping God because that's the only way they can feel. Then they find who they really are. It's not the hardened person on the outside, but it's really the real person on the inside.

DEREK CHIAMPAS: I think that soul is the currency for dealing with the Devil. You sell your soul and you get something great in return – except then you are going to have to serve an eternity of damnation.

VAN SANDWICK: Soul is a muscle and some people, instead of expressing their soul, they go to church and they pray to God and they believe in God and this is how they feel that they are expressing their soul, and they are trying to feel happy. But then there are some people who go to church and still feel miserable.

ANN SAWYER: There are people who go to church because they go to church to say they go to church. But I visited some churches with my youth group, and if you ever go to one of those extremely active, predominantly African-American gospel churches, they are really getting into it, and it really seems like they are expressing themselves. There are literally people breakdancing in the aisle while they are singing. Who knows? At that point they might not even be thinking about being at church. They might just be thinking about what color the sky is and loving it.

NATHAN WORCESTER: Sometimes in a church or a religious building of some sort, it doesn't matter how visible the soulfulness is. For example, I go to a church that is predominantly old white people and they are quiet and not breakdancing. But they reach out in much more quiet but still soulful ways.

CHRISSY DELACOTTA: A few years ago, I was in Maine at this absolutely beautiful church for Easter mass. There was a choir, and they were singing this amazing hymn. I don't even know what happened, but I felt touched by the whole religious experience. I don't even know if I believe in it yet, but something in that moment made me want to believe in everything again. I think that was pretty soulful.

OSCAR BROWN, JR.: I started hearing about soul in church, of course. It was an aspect of the Holy Ghost, which was a part of the trilogy of our Father, Son and Holy Ghost. Soul was a spiritual component of life that everybody had. It was always sort of a mystical thing, I think intentionally so, because it was something you couldn't put your finger on. It was that part of you that continued after the rest of you was gone. That was the part that went to Heaven and had an existence that was extraterrestrial and extraordinary. That was the first time I started hearing about soul.

TOM BURRELL: Soul had been a term that I was familiar with in a religious context. Just that your soul was going someplace after your body was no longer functioning, alive, and I guess I bought into that for a minute, but that was basically it.

DAVID BLOOM: So you wouldn't consider yourself growing up with a strong sense of religion?

TOM BURRELL: I actually grew up with a strong sense of religion at certain points in my life. I went through a lot of different changes as relates to religion. For some reason I, along with a couple of other people in the neighborhood, we each just kind of took it upon ourselves to do a comparative study of religion by going to different kinds of churches and other institutions. I have no idea where we got that from. It didn't come from reading. We spent a little while over at Prairie Avenue Baptist Church and then we'd go over to Greater Tabernacle Church of Christ, which was the Sanctified church. Then we would head out to Winnetka, to the Bahai Temple, and we would go to Catholic church. I have no idea what the hell we were doing.

DAVID BLOOM: How old were you when you were touring different churches?

TOM BURRELL: About eight or nine years old.

DAVID BLOOM: Really? Who was taking you to them?

TOM BURRELL: Nobody was. We were taking ourselves. Mostly Sunday schools. We were taking ourselves. Every Sunday we put on our wing-tipped, scotch-grained, double-knit outer soles, offset heels, with our argyle socks, and our three-way suits. You know what three-way suits were? You had the vest and the coat and two pair of pants, and you could switch the pair of pants and you could flip the vest, the vest was reversible. And we had our Mr. B. collars for our hair and our knit ties, like this, and our stingy brim hats, and of course it was stingy brim because the brim was about an inch, and we'd head out. We'd head out to various schools. There were no parents. No parents involved at all. They just sent us off and that's what we did.

I don't know if we were searching for religion. I don't know what the hell we were doing. I know it gave us a chance to dress up, but we weren't looking for girls because we were too young for that; I don't think we were thinking about that. I don't remember any girls from Sunday school. I don't know what we were doing. But anyway, I just know that I didn't stay.

CHRISTIAN STEINBARTH: You can have a soul but not believe in God. It does not really have to be associated with any religion.

STUDS TERKEL: You're talking to an agnostic. An agnostic, as you know, is a cowardly atheist. However, do I believe in a certain kind of god? Yes, I suppose I do. Depends how you interpret God. Anthropomorphic being, no. He, she, it – a force of some sort, you know. If you want to be anthropomorphic about it, God is described as a white male, right? Or there is, of course, the African interpretation too, the black male. Has anyone thought of God as a woman? And suppose God was gay, let's talk about that. Let's talk about Jesus Christ. Now, who was he? What was his color? Was he white? He, I said. Could it be a she?

Now a big question that would come up today, especially with the subject of gay and lesbian life, I suppose – this all concerns soul by the way, indirectly – suppose Jesus Christ were a gay person? Would that alter the Sermon on the Mount, what he said? Would that alter love thine enemy, love thy neighbor? Would that alter the parable of the seven little fishes and five loaves of bread?

BOB WILLEMS: I grew up in a very Catholic family. I was an altar boy and I went to church on Sundays, the whole works. I was raised at a time when the Catholic church had just come to grips with embracing the New Testament rather than the Old Testament. I think even today people into Catholicism are much more attached to the Ten Commandments, and we have laws, and here's the way things are, and it's cut and dried.

The New Testament presents this other view, which is you can screw up everything else in the world, you can do whatever you want, and just love. Love. The whole thing is about love. I grew up in that church, and the priests that were influential in my upbringing and the people who I knew through my church were about that, and they got that. That was the important thing to me.

ANDREA COSNOWSKY: When I thought about becoming a rabbi in high school, it was very different than when I thought about becoming a rabbi later on. First of all, I grew up Conservative. To be a Conservative rabbi, it just looked like I'd be doing endless amounts of services. As a high school student, my perception was all I did was go to services, and it was long hours. When I was in my twenties, I was looking through mature eyes at what it meant to really be a rabbi. Services are important, but that's just one small facet. I really saw becoming a rabbi as service to the Jewish people but also to all mankind – or humankind to be more politically correct.

DAVID BLOOM: Has anything changed regarding your soul after you became a rabbi?

ANDREA COSNOWSKY: Now that I am a rabbi and in a real position, I understand that it's really about touching people one person at a time. Where I thought I'd be touching huge amounts of people as a rabbi in front of a big congregation, I find that my sermons don't change people as much as my touch does at the hospital bed, or my presence in a house of mourning, or just sitting next to a bat/bar mitzvah child on their big day. And they're nervous, and I say to them, "You're going to be great." Those are the moments where lives are touched more so than on Yom Kippur when everybody's here that wouldn't normally be here, and they're listening to a sermon.

I think I had this idea that I would be touching people on a big scale where it's really a one to one process. It's more of I am the vessel, and I will let God work through me to bring people closer to God. It's really not about me anymore. It's really about I'm here to be of service. I'm here as the vessel of God.

STUDS TERKEL: In the civil liberties movement in the African-American community, almost all of the leaders are ministers: Rev. Martin Luther King, Rev. Ralph Abernathy, Rev. Young – Andrew Young, Rev. James Bevel, Rev. Jesse Jackson, you see, Rev. C. T. Vivian. So when we come to soul, the church in African American life played a bigger role than for any other people – because the church was also the center, not only of religion, but the social center, the political center. The hope was there.

DAVID BLOOM: On your radio program you introduced the great gospel singer Mahalia Jackson to the white world. Obviously, she had a strong religiosity in her whole being. Do you think her emotions and soulfulness were inextricably connected to her religiosity?

STUDS TERKEL: Well, Mahalia happened to be gifted with a remarkable voice and a way of expressing herself. So we had a very funny relationship because she knew I was a skeptic and I was an agnostic, and so sometimes she would act this out for me. When she'd sing a song, she'd imitate me and say, "Baby, you got me going, you got me going." And she'd say, "If I could save his soul, oh that'd be good." I'd say, "Mahalia, I'm beyond salvation, but if anybody can, you can."

> *Religion is the sigh of the oppressed creature, the heart of a heartless world, and the soul of soulless conditions. It is the opium of the people.*
>
> *-Karl Marx*

BILL HORBERG: I don't think of the soul in religious terms because I think of religion as the institutionalization of a certain way that communities form to discuss the phenomenology of the world and how they can try to find some shared way of describing the mysterious.

> *Frisbeetarianism is the belief that when you die, your soul goes up on the roof and gets stuck.*
>
> *-George Carlin*

OSCAR BROWN, JR.: I remember by the time I got into college, I went to DePaul. It was a Catholic school, and they had courses in logic. One of the things they said was animals didn't have souls. "How do you know?" was my question. They never could answer that. You have to take that on faith that only human beings have souls. It's convenient to say that for yourself, but how do you know? You can't show me mine. If you can't define it beyond my just accepting an explanation by faith, then why must I have faith that you know what another creature's spiritual life might be? That was one of my arguments there, and I was becoming leftist and atheist in my thought. I really didn't have too much to do with soul at that point.

What actually brought me back into that concept was my sincere determination to prove to the world that God was a hoax and there could not be such a thing. As I set out to accomplish that, I had to first of all create a concept of God that I was going to destroy. If I was going to be honest about it, it had to be a pretty comprehensive concept. It had to cover all the corners. There could be no gaps. I would build the concept to destroy – but no, that wasn't enough. There had to be more. I had to build it beyond that. Finally, it got to the point where the concept grew so large that questioning it became ridiculous. Who am I and what am I doing here? Obviously, the thing that I am seeking is so powerful that if there wasn't such a thing, there ought to be. Since there ought to be, there is. You just have to accept that.

My whole concept of that has changed through the years. Now I've come to the conclusion that gravity is God in disguise. Everything we do is predicated on the restrictions and freedoms that gravity gives us. We have to have strength to deal with that. We have to have balance in order to deal with that. We have to worship it. We have to give up six or eight hours every day just to replenish that, or it takes us down. We don't fall apart or go to pieces or fly away. We just go down. So my whole concept of how the Almighty expresses and appears manifest has changed. It's not an anthropomorphic concept of God in which I think of man made in God's image. Of course, man is made in God's image. If I think you up, I made the image. You are my creation.

ANDREA COSNOWSKY: My concept of God has changed over the years. First of all, I've grown up and I've seen more, so I have a different understanding of God and God's role in my life. I think I went through a period of time where I thought God was an interventionist God, where

God could reach into my life and rearrange things if I prayed hard enough or if I was good enough. Today I don't perceive God on that level. I believe that the laws of nature are in place – perhaps put there by God, perhaps by evolution. I don't want to get into that controversy. More important is this idea that God is loving, and no matter what happens in my life, God's presence is accessible to me.

BILL KURTIS: Among many Indian cultures, soul and religion probably are the same thing, because they lived on the land and had a food source. They worshiped the buffalo. They worshiped the spirit inside the buffalo: the spirit inside every living thing. They would take it to survive and sustain themselves and their family, but they would pray and give thanks to that spirit for helping them. And they used everything. They were nomadic so they couldn't acquire a lot of material goods. And they would move across the land following the buffalo. They were very warlike, which we forget about. We think about the wonderful Indian out there looking at the sky and developing his religion. But they fought each other an awful lot and that's why they resisted the United States when we were trying to move west. And it was a violent resistance.

But they had time to develop a religion. They had creation theories, they had myths and legends which contributed to the belief in a Great Spirit. Theirs just happens to be very useful to us today because they saw the spirit and had respect for the world in which they lived: grass, water, the elements of wind, sun and the living things that existed within it. I tend to gravitate back toward that religion more than any others. Some people choose Buddhism, Catholicism, statues. I like the natural world. It's not pagan in my mind; it's very wise.

ANDREA COSNOWSKY: Religion is man-made and spirituality is God-made. For people who can't access the divine within themselves, they hedge their bets, if you will. For those who believe that it's not about going to synagogue and getting your card punched to say, "Look, I've done what I'm supposed to do," and they're doing what they're supposed to do, it means trying to be the best person they can be. Not stealing, not hurting each other, and not getting in the way as much as we can.

We're human beings, so we're going to make mistakes. We're going to cause chaos. We're going to step on each other's toes, but it's our ability to try to do the best we can. That's where the spirit is. So soul is what dictates my behavior, and religion is when I try to dictate other people's behavior.

I think we as individuals, in whatever country we're in, might be better off tending to our own souls than to our neighbors'.

SOUL AND YOU

Beyond its religious significance, the word "soul" pertains to a person's individuality. Everyone has his or her own soul, whether they acknowledge its existence or not. Even in the absence of normal cognition, that unique spirit does not vanish. As long as a person is alive, their soul lives – and possibly survives forever. Souls evolve, develop complexity, and visibly disappear only upon death.

Souls need company, many people say, because souls prefer happiness to loneliness. Some souls are likable, others not so much. Obstacles can block the development of soulfulness, but sometimes soul grows best when it's impeded. Then there's the question most children ponder: Do animals have souls?

Souls go through a life cycle, from birth until death. People in this chapter talk about newborns and how their souls flourish as their bodies grow. They tell stories about soulful childhoods as well as influences on their souls' progress. And finally, they discuss death: their parents', their friends' and their own.

Radu Florin

INDIVIDUALITY: THE ESSENCE OF BEING HUMAN

The wealth of a soul is measured by how much it can feel; its poverty by how little.

-William R. Alger

ZACK GRAHAM: The first time I felt my soul was during a basketball game. I was at the free-throw line. I was about zero for twelve at the free-throw line, and I was having a bad day. I really wasn't feeling it. The commissioner of the basketball league that I was playing in, he really didn't like me, because his kid was on his team, and he wanted his team to beat every other team. He really wanted me to miss the shot, because if I had made the shot we would have won the game. I dribbled the ball, and I was ready to shoot, and I looked at him. He gives me this look like "miss, miss, miss." Then all of a sudden, everything goes away. I guess it was just the soul that came out of me, because I shot, the ball sank, and I felt it go all the way in. We won the game. That was the first time I consciously felt that something had taken over. I used some of that force to really help my team win the game and help myself develop. I found out a lot about myself during that moment.

DAVID BLOOM: My dad had Alzheimer's and I really didn't have a conversation with him for the last eight years. We'd take a walk and he would say hello to everybody like he knew them. It really hit me at the time that cognition can only go so far, and really not far at all.

BOB WILLEMS: It also says something about the pervasiveness of the soul. You can do a lot of things to the body of the human or the physical manifestation of what you are as a person, or your cognition, something that people prize as the most important thing in their lives. But the soul is untouchable. The mind is a minor concern for the soul. The soul is operating on a level that's unfazed by any of these details.

ELSA MORA: I think soul is very unique, and it was something that was not there forever. Soul is something that started happening to people over years and years and years of evolution of accumulation of experiences. In the end, it's not something completely personal; it's something related to the universe, and the universe is people. These experiences and all the things that happen around you and all the things that you make happen, that's the way I feel about soul. Without soul, you're nothing. You're a piece of meat.

DON MEADE: Each soul is an individual soul. You are you. Now, do you spend your life being you? Or when do you discover that you are you? And when you discover, what do you do after that? You go back to the mirror. Do you like what you see when you go look in the mirror? Some people don't. And guess what? They don't like nobody else all day long. Or forever, some of them. We got people who like dogs better than they do people. You know, buy his dog a mink coat. He wouldn't even buy himself one. Where do we put priorities at?

CHARLES JAFFE: The essence of being human is what we're talking about, about the unique property and vitality of being human at its core.

DAVID BLOOM: Do creatures other than human beings have soul?

RICK KOGAN: Do I think that a lion or a tiger has soul? I do not. I do not. I'm not one of these tree-hugging characters. I don't think we should kill any animals for any reason, but I do not think that it's all part of the same thing. They may have some sort of different thing, that's of a different definition. They communicate in different ways. It's individualistic.

STUDS TERKEL: I don't have any pets, but what about a cat or a dog? What about the lion or the tiger or the elephant? What about those in the cages? If I'm to be an animal rights advocate (I'm not), what about those in the zoo? Do animals have a soul? When I say animals, we're animals, we're the top rung and that's questionable, by the way. I don't know any member of the animal kingdom outside of our species who makes war just for making war's sake. They do it to survive, one way or another. They eat other animals, they attack, but just for the hell of it as the human race does, that's something else. So I'm not sure we're the top rung of the animal kingdom.

DAVID BLOOM: Would you say, when someone is soulful, it's mandatory that they're an individual?

NATHAN WORCESTER: I think so. Absolutely. I think that to be soulful, you do have an individual point of view. It has to be from your perspective. What makes us all different is our soul. Otherwise we'll just be atoms pushed together in a very random way.

CHARLES JAFFE: You're talking about an essential, core, motivating, organizing quality of a person: the uniqueness of a person, a particular emotional quality. We talk about a characteristic set of behaviors or beliefs, but when you put it in terms of soul, you're really capturing a powerful, emotional ambiance that is expressed in those characteristic patterns of people. In the search that people go through in a psychoanalyst's office, what we follow together is their range of emotion. Emotion and meaning and motivation are all very, very closely related concepts, so all of that is a search for their soul and an expression of their soul or soulfulness.

ANDREA COSNOWSKY: Individuality can only exist in a larger context which is that if I go and live at the top of a mountain and I'm not part of a community, then my individuality is not worth much.

I don't believe we were meant to live alone. It's important to have our quiet time and to reflect, but that reflection should fuel us to go become better members of our society and our community.

BILL KURTIS: Well, soul is reality; it is truth. It is something that doesn't have a language. It's a feeling. It comes from inside, and each of us has that soul. It can be expressed in any number of ways. Your talent is essentially your tool of expression and soul will drive it, but the minute you get away from the reality of truth within you, then you get in trouble. You lose that focus and that soul. That means that if you want to be a trumpet player and wind up being an accountant, you're not happy.

What we value, and I mean everyone in every profession, I think, is originality: something we hear for the first time that hasn't been done any other way. You will go to art school and you will learn how to be an artist. You'll go to music school and you'll learn the notes and you'll learn how everybody else plays. But until you kind of jump off the cliff and use these tools as your own, you're not in an area of true originality where you will be one, happy, and two, successful. It's learning and appreciating the system and the institutions – but do it yourself. Don't be like someone else. Only you possess this thing within you. As Gandhi said, "Be the change you wish to see in the world." Be yourself.

RICK KOGAN: This world these days, to my mind, is moving on some sort of surface level. There's no emotional traction going on. It's all like some sort of Electro-Glide thing and you want to go through your life as smoothly as possible. And life will throw you. I don't care whose life it is. It'll throw you up and down, if you let it. If you let it! But what most people seem to me, in my humble opinion, to do is start compressing that as soon as they can into this area that is undeniably comfortable. And I don't begrudge people doing this. But their definition becomes so limited, so out of touch with the real world, as to kind of make me sad.

Are you able to be soulful as a banker? Absolutely. Look at someone like hmm… I don't know any bankers. But what I'm saying is it's always so easy to attach the label "soulful" to an artist. I think that is so arrogant. I think that is so arrogant and unfair to think that someone working at a punch-press, someone working as a bus-boy, because they're not exploring some "higher art," has an inability to be soulful.

BARRETT DOSS: Someone who's soulful is someone who usually doesn't really ever seem to be pessimistic or act in a way that makes people feel unhappy. They just act in a way so that everyone's happy, I would say. They're just trying to be themselves and be expressive. That's what makes them happy, so they're soulful.

TOM BREWER: You can be also be soulful if you're unhappy. I don't think B.B. King was always happy when he was singing the blues, but I think he did it with soul.

TOM BURRELL: What you are basically talking about is getting down to who you are and what matters to you, what makes you, you. I don't think you can really be expressive and caring unless you have some other sense of who you really are, and so I think there is a tremendous correlation. They are almost overlaid, the issue between individuality and soulfulness.

You know, if you have ever related to music, there is only one James Brown, there can only be one James Brown. You are talking about imperfect beings, because we all are; it's just how are you good and what are you contributing. What are you doing that makes it worthwhile to occupy space on the planet?

DAVID BLOOM: Can you be soulful without being an individual?

CLIFF COLNOT: In its most pure, unadulterated form, individuality is incompatible with soulfulness. However, I think individuals who are soulful can remain their own person and retain their individual voice, but I do not think that's easy nor do I think it's common. To be clearer about it, I don't think that the individuality of Solomon Burke and Aretha Franklin and Otis Redding was incidental at all to the profoundness of the soul music movement in the 1960s. What I believe is that those particular individuals were able to remain humble and remain in awe of something greater than their own individuality while presenting their individuality in a very powerful, unadulterated way. They were powerfully and uniquely individual, but they were well aware of something greater than their own individuality.

ZACK GRAHAM: Soul is something you're born with and something you die with. How you use it and how you find it and what you use it for are things that can only be judged by the period of your lifetime. Each individual uses their soul differently. Each individual's soul is differently powerful. You can sense that, and it's something that you just can't teach.

Theo Fitzhug

THE BIRTH OF A SOUL

DAVID BLOOM: Do you think people are born with soul?

CHRISSY DELACOTTA: I think everybody is born with a new soul. Your soul is who you are. As you grow older and as you get closer toward death, you try to get closer to who you really are, who or what your real soul is.

STUDS TERKEL: Once we're born, depends how we're born. Are we born in poverty, are we born in absolute despair? Or are we born in luxury? Are we born in what you might call, not affluent, but just an ordinary family? A lot depends on the circumstance of your birth and what happens to you after you're born.

BILL HORBERG: In some profound way, I would say as an adult, the deepest realization, manifestation, connection I've had to soul has been in the moment of the birth of each of my children. I felt, standing in the room when my first son was born and greeting this other person and recognizing him, that there was already a real developed person there, a sense of self, a sense of personality. It was an indescribable moment.

ELSA MORA: I have a little baby, and I'm expecting another one. That's something really important. That's something that has made me feel like somebody with a bigger soul. Why? Because imagine there is somebody that you are responsible for. Soul has a lot to do with connections with things around you. Your connect with your kids is amazing, because there is nothing to do. That's your kid. You have to give them the best you can. It doesn't matter if they are adopted and you brought them from China, it doesn't matter. It's just something important in your life that you have to give a lot to.

PATTI VASQUEZ: I made a person, I did. Some of you have made a person, some of you have made people. One woman told me she made ten people. That's just overachieving: Can you try finding a parking spot? Wrong.

It took me three years to get my bun in the oven, and I know people will say oh, the father had something to do with it. Yeah, well, when push comes to shove I did all the pushing. He did what he always does which included some pushing and shoving but not the kind of pushing this mama had to do, okay.

I love this new life, I do, and my son is admirable; he's six months old. My brain is still shrinking with the idea that he's teething today, he's adorable though. He's got a little penis and everything. I knew that he would, but I just had never seen one from scratch before.

That's the thing, everything feels like it's starting from scratch, it really does, and I had a life before this new life, you know. Now I have no life but it's still our life and it's not a bad life. This new life is a little tired, and cluttered, and messy, and tired, and soggy, and sexless, and tired and stained - and not because of the sex and yet really because of the sex.

ELSA MORA: When I was pregnant the first time, I felt like wow, this is amazing. I'm going to have a baby, but that baby is part of my body. It's inside me, so I was thinking that baby is somebody else. It is a new person, but I feel in same way that it's also me. I'm feeling this person in many ways, not only physically but with my mind. I'm imagining the way she's going to be. I'm like a closet. You know? I'm containing this new life, and I felt great about that. Like this is amazing what human nature is.

BILL HORBERG: My daughter who is now two years old, Natalie: just seeing her arrive and seeing her come into our life as this total force of nature, and how she has been able to change and affect us through her soul - she's just a little two-year-old, twenty-two pounds, nothing - and yet the strength of what's inside her and the strength of what speaks to everybody around her, in her immediate family and the people that she meets with in her life, to me it's just been a window into something truly mysterious.

DAVID BLOOM: Are babies born with the full potential to realize their soul?

PHILLIP VERNA: You're born with a soul but it's hard to know when it's going to show and be manifested. I mean, you can be really naturally soulful, or you can not have soulfulness unless something really stimulates it.

ANN SAWYER: You can be born with a soul but I think it's a skill. You might necessarily know that it's there and you don't know until you exercise it and you work at it. And maybe you'll never realize it. Maybe somebody else will point it out to you and then you'll plan it out.

RICK KOGAN: You want to see soul? Go look in the eyes of a newborn child, 'cause that's where it is. And the world is going to conspire to destroy that, or at least repress it. You hope that somehow these little babies are lucky enough to have an environment as they grow up that tries to nurture (they're not trying to nurture soul, they're trying to nurture whatever "qualities" the baby has, as they grow up). The point is: Nurture away, but don't repress with this pragmatic attitude that you are somehow going to be a failure as a human being unless you get into this school, unless you have this kind of job, unless you marry this kind of woman (or man), unless you have this kind of baby, unless you live in this kind of place. That is what's so screwed up about this country. Does someone have less soul or less success if they live in the Austin neighborhood than on Astor Street?

ANDREA COSNOWSKY: I believe that when you look into a baby's eyes – if you've ever held a newborn baby – you can look and see there is a soul inside this child that is absolutely pure and has probably the most close connection to God. I watched the eyelids of my newborn son, and I realized my son was dreaming, but I couldn't possibly imagine what he could be dreaming about. He'd only been on earth a few days. What could he have been dreaming? That tells me that there was a connection or a communication happening on some level for him that had to transcend this world.

I believe that what happens to us is that the farther away from God we get, we teach each other for better or for worse what we hope will be the skills that our kids need. I think what we're teaching them is how to disconnect from our souls. Our job as human beings is to clear away what blocks us from that God connection that we had at a few days old and get back to our truest selves.

Felix Koutchinski

THE GROWTH OF A SOUL

There can be no keener revelation of a society's soul than the way in which it treats its children.

-Nelson Mandela

BILL KURTIS: Where do we build character these days? That's something I worry about. Where does a child, going through our system of schooling, have an opportunity to achieve those little successes that really will point him in the right direction after school? I think children have a natural soul because they don't have all the burdens of responsibilities. But they lose it about age twelve, just when they're becoming teenagers and they start wanting to impress other people.

ELSA MORA: It is very funny in this country how you try to control the life of your children. I want them to be good, to be this and that. You just need one thing: You need to create the conditions for them to be happy with themselves. Create the condition for them to feel free to explore, to understand things, to go out and feel comfortable with other people. Sometimes you want to protect them so much that, in the end, they are afraid. I want to do this opposite with my girl.

It is hard, because this is a strong culture. I want her to grow up comfortable with the way she looks, she sees herself. I don't want her to suffer things that are not important in life, so that's how I combine everything in my work, in my life, my role as a mother, wife, sister, and everything. I try to put it all together in that way, like just go ahead, be open, flexible, enjoy life. Life is short, so that little time is the most important thing that you have. Don't waste it. Do the best you can, and that's it. That's the point. Just open your soul, fill it up with many good things, and you'll be happy.

DON MEADE: I came up in a time where I saw the last of the horse and buggy and the first of the electric refrigerator. That was all in my time, okay? I remember when you carried fifty pounds of ice on your back up three flights of a six-flat — and when you got home, it was melted. All my teachers were from my mother and father's generation. I learned politics from my grandfather. I learned religion from my grandmother. All of those things. But that came from a generation far away from me. If those people were alive today, they'd be a hundred and sixteen, a hundred and twenty years old. That's my bunch. That was my learning tree. That was my training ground.

RICK KOGAN: I look back on my childhood as the most glorious thing. I think I'm probably the last generation of Chicago kids and maybe all big-city kids who could begin the day in the summer time with "Bye, Ma!" And instead of being worried about where were you going, her only answer was, "Be home before it gets dark!" So you had this freedom to go explore the world around you. First it was indeed your one little block, then it was a bigger block, then it became the entire city! Yeah, I played ball, I played all sorts of little games. But that sort of exploration was really something. To have fifty cents and take the bus downtown and just wander around and if you saw someone, go, "Hi, what do you do? Why are you wearing that funny hat? Why are you doing this? Why are you doing that?"

My dad was a newspaper man and my mom was a public relations director for the Art Institute. So I had the glorious opportunity to have our house filled with artists. Most of them, I must admit, were really unpretentious: people like Nelson Algren, Studs Terkel, Winn Stracke, Willard Motley, or this guy called "Quoizette The Clairvoyant," who was supposed to be able to tell the future. We would hide in the apartment and I would go, "Where's my brother?" And he'd seem to go into this trance. "Your brother is... under the bed." And even at eight, I'd go, "No, he's in a closet! What kind of a clairvoyant are you!?"

This was a freewheeling kind of crowd who spoke their minds, who maybe drank too much, maybe smoked too much. But when it came to the business of talking to one another about things that they thought were important, and in a really passionate way, I remember – you know, most kids have memories of "My parents used to scream at each other, and our house was always filled with noise." The louder it got in our house, when Mark and I were kids, the more you wanted to hear what was going on because it was not conflict. It was passion, it was interest. It was passion directed at the right things. It was genuine. To hear Winn Stracke, even a little half in the bag, singing "The 43rd Ward" on our back porch, I can still hear it! And I swear to you, I still sort of tingle about it, 'cause he sat on the railing of our second-story porch, and Winn was a huge man, and playing that guitar the way he played it with his booming voice, any minute this man could fall off! He never fell off.

People like Mortimer Adler, who founded the Great Books, would come over and my dad would say, "Now, don't go up and ask him if he's the smartest man in the world." And of course, we'd go up and ask him, "Are you the smartest man in the world?" And he'd say, "Who told you that?!" But then what he would do (and I don't see people doing this much, when I go to friends' houses these days), he took a seven and an eight-year-old off in the corner and just talked to us! What did he say exactly? I'm not sure, but I remember just being rapt in attention.

When the young Mort Sahl came over in the '60s, (my father used to cover a lot of comedy and theater) we answered the door (we were always allowed to answer the door), and we said, "Hi, who are you?" And he said, "I'm the Man From Mars." And we went, "Oh, God, oh, so cool!" And he goes, "Who are you?" And we said, "Rick and Mark." And he goes, "No, you're not. You're Strelka and Belka, the two dogs the Russians have sent off into space!" For a year, we only called ourselves Strelka and Belka.

I remember winter afternoons in our living room when I would come to my father and ask something like, "Dad, who was Spartacus?" And my father, instead of saying, "Well, I don't know," would take the Encyclopedia Britannica off the shelves and say, "Here, this is who Spartacus was." And I would read all about that. Another thing that he used to do was play for us two little kids his amazing collection of old records (78's of Louis Armstrong and The Hot Five) and explain to us – not just say, "Here, shut up, you guys," or "Here, watch TV," he'd explain to us how Louis

Armstrong was such a transcendent musician and player, and that when they made these sort of primitive recordings, the band was in one room and they had to put him in another room across the hall when he played his cornet because it would just destroy the whole sound, because he was just so amazing.

My father would play Billie Holiday, which moved me in a strange way at a very young age; I just felt there was something in that music that touched me. But then again, my father was able to tell me how he was in love with Billie Holiday when he was a young reporter in Chicago and how he would, after work, go see her perform. And I was fascinated that my father was in this room, admitting to being in love with a black woman who sang songs. My mother was not black and did not sing songs. And I was thinking this is really pretty amazing!

Then, apropos of nothing, he would take out his violin (because he was a little, first-generation Jewish kid who took violin lessons). And he would put on show tunes, and he would play along with the show tunes – you know, *Damn Yankees*, *Pajama Game*. And I, in retrospect maybe more so than I did then, thought it was a blast! Here was my father, showing me a side of himself that I didn't see other fathers showing to their kids. You know, I thought to myself, "Well, maybe this happens in the privacy of their own homes." But, right around that time, I learned that this was not what parents did. This was the '50s, early '60s. Parents were like the guy on *Leave It To Beaver* and *The Donna Reed Show*. They were authority figures, who were the people who told you what to do, who in a way did that whole "repression of…" And my father seemed, on the other hand, to be expressing himself in a way that fathers did not do in those days.

This was a totally different generation. We didn't have soccer practice! There were no soccer moms! There was none of that stuff. But at least at my house, there was the intimation, if not the nurturing, of a kind of freedom. Certainly, we had to behave or we'd be spanked, but there wasn't a lot of "No, don't bother your dad; he's listening to *The Pajama Game*," or "Don't bother your dad; he's remembering being in love with Billie Holiday!" He was sharing this, with little kids. And I can't really evoke how jarring it might have been. I'm thinking, "You father is telling you he's in love with a black woman who's singing on this record and your mom is this white woman who…" Now, I get it totally! Then, it was probably very mysterious to me. But there was something about it that I appreciated and, certainly, I appreciate it now.

BOB WILLEMS: I grew up in the suburbs of Chicago, a western suburb called Riverside. It's a relatively small suburb but pretty solidly at the time middle, upper middle class. I was an only child. We had a small family there. Growing up in the suburbs was an interesting experience because you can live in isolation from a lot of things in the world. In fact, you can argue that the suburbs are designed in some ways to promote that sort of thing. But I was fortunate enough to have a family that was very conscious about exposing me to different things. Even in eighth grade I was suddenly aware of the fact that this world that I'm in here is not like the broader world. We'd go to the city to do something like see a ball game, and I'm like, "Wow. What is this? This is not like the stuff that I'm surrounded by day to day."

When I was deciding where to go to high school, I was looking all over the Chicago area and checked out Saint Ignatius College Prep, which was a West Side city high school. I thought it was a great place to go, both academically but also because it was a school where I could study with kids from all different backgrounds, all different ethnicities, and really being pretty much on the playing field with all of them. They all were there to study and go through the high school experience together. Having to depart the suburbs, I don't really feel a great attachment to them.

DON MEADE: I was born and raised in Joliet, Illinois, during the Great Depression. In fact, I was born a year before the Depression. Interesting time, bittersweet time. I think that anyone that lived through that Depression will live with those scars. They were a challenging time, a time of survival socially, economically, politically, musically – probably one of the better times musically. I learned at an early age. I played in a symphony orchestra at eight years old: children's orchestra at Joliet. We were fortunate to have a WPA band. It would go around all the schools, and the best kids were put into the city orchestra.

In 1940 we had an Atwater Kent radio and I remember a Friday night broadcast of Basie Band. There was tune called "Down For Double." And it just, you wouldn't believe how it went right to the heart of my soul. I went to school every day and my teacher told me if I hum that tune one more time, I was kicked out of school. I would sit up right in middle of class and go dope dope de re rop ba dope dope de re rop ba.

I heard the tune again, ironically, December 7, 1941, the day they bombed Pearl Harbor. That was the day before my thirteenth birthday. My birthday was Monday morning, 8th of December and they bombed Pearl Harbor 7th of December. I had my birthday party that Sunday afternoon. And would you know it, my mother had bought that record, Count Basie's "Down For Double." It was strange because the 8th of December is really a Catholic holiday called Feast of Immaculate Conception. That got me into trouble once, because my 8th grade teacher had birthday things for all of the students and she would tell you whether your birthday is famous or not. Well, I'd never heard of "immaculate conception" before. So I said, "Well, maybe I'm the immaculate conception." Oh, that got me into a little trouble but it was good trouble because that was the beginning of me being very particular about where I place the words and meanings.

I was fortunate enough to be reared in the multi-ethnic community. It was Italians, Jewish people, Mexicans, Gypsies, everything, everybody. Italian probably was my first language because I couldn't speak until I was six. I just stuttered so bad, I couldn't get the words out. My trachea was sitting on my windpipe and I couldn't get my voice through. We lived across the street from an Italian opera singer, Dominick Bayone, and he told my grandfather to send me over on Thursdays and Saturdays to teach me voice lessons. Kids used to laugh. I became very proficient at throwing rocks. In fact, I could knock you out a block away. I made it past that because I had a strong will. I knew then, or had a good idea then, what I'd be doing now. And I always told kids: I'm going to know Nat King Cole. I'm going to know Ella Fitzgerald. I'm going to know Artie Shaw, all of those people. I've done all of those things. I did that. I sacrificed my whole childhood. I didn't want one so I didn't pursue one. I moved on.

TED COHEN: My dad was a handsome guy, businessman. Been in the Army for over two years while I was a little kid. He looked to me like somebody who really knew what he was doing. I thought he was very intelligent. He was one of the few guys I knew who made a living mostly with his brains. I admired the farmers. They could do stuff I couldn't do, but my dad did other stuff. He sold insurance. He lent money. He arranged business deals and stuff. He seemed to me to know a lot. He was very reliable. He was one of those fathers who had kind of an idea of what his kid would do but wasn't going to push it. He was a big support all the time. Whatever you want to do, that's okay. "Well, I think what I'm going to do is so unlike what you do that I'll move away and never see you again." He said, "That's okay too."

I was smaller than all the other boys. They were farm boys. They were kind of strong and knew how to do physical, manual things that I couldn't do. I had a special disability in that regard. I'm a product of the American public school system in one of its more benighted phases. They thought that if you had a kid who learned what you were teaching him and was getting bored, the right thing to do was to put him in another grade. This happened to me a couple of times. Shouldn't do that with kids in school. I'll tell you what happens. You take a kid in kindergarten, first grade, second grade, third grade, and the kid's learning everything without any trouble and sitting there and getting bored. You put him in the next grade, and after four weeks he'll be sitting there bored. The difference will be that he's no longer in the right age group.

How did all this skipping affect my social scene? It was bad. Only during the last, I would say, two, three months of my school career was I as tall as any girl in my class. That's not good when you're a young boy and you're trying to figure out what's what. Music was good, because I learned to play early. Socially no, I was thought of as the odd little kid who was smart, but a girl wouldn't want to go out with him, and she'd be taller than he was. I couldn't drive because I was too young to get a driver's license. Even if you would go out with her, you couldn't go anywhere.

I had friends, boys I ran around with and did stuff with. It was great growing up in a small town. It never even occurred to me until I was about fifty years old that when I was a kid, I could spend weeks without ever seeing a human being I didn't know. People who live in a city don't understand what that kind of life is like. In the end, it can be kind of claustrophobic and not everybody can stand it. I don't think I could stand it for a lifetime. When you're a kid that's not bad. I knew the blacksmith. I knew the woman who ran the restaurant. I knew the postmaster. I knew everybody. I talked to people and hung out with people, and they kind of liked me. I was a relatively likable kid, so I wasn't unhappy.

I had an experience once, I remember. I went into my grandfather's general store one day after school when I was about thirteen, with these farmers. It was the winter, so they came in and sat around this potbellied stove and did what farmers do, which is talk and drag in mud. One of them said to me, "Do you know how to figure a square root?" I said, "As a matter of fact, yes I do." I had a math teacher, a crazy bastard who had taught us how to do this. It's a largely worthless skill, but he taught me how to do it. This guy said, "Can you do this? We know how many square feet there are in an acre, but we don't know what the dimensions would be." So I did it. They liked me for that. I liked being able to do it.

ELSA MORA: I grew up in Cuba, in a very extreme atmosphere. A lot of violence and poverty and many problems, but I had a very special mother, very strong person, very positive. Sometimes we felt bad about not having shoes or things like that, and my mom always said, "You know what? That's not important. You have a pair of shoes tomorrow. The most important thing is something here, something that happens in your head. All the things that you have here, that's what's going to save you."

I remember once, for example, I went to my school. I didn't have socks, because my mom couldn't afford that. All the children were like, "Why aren't you wearing socks? That's not nice," because that was the rule in the school. I remember I said something like, "No, the problem is that I have a problem with my feet, some condition that I can't wear things like that." I mean, I was feeling ashamed of not having socks.

When I told my mom the story, she said, "Look Elsa, don't ever feel sorry about not having material things. That's not important. If one day you are insensitive or you do something bad to another person, and they ask you why you do that, you can feel bad about that, because that's something that's really important. Don't ever worry about material things."

DAVE LIEBMAN: I had polio at three years old, 1949, the last big epidemic. From what I understand, it was considered like what AIDS was at the beginning. People would cross the street and not come near the house, that kind of thing. I was in hospital for over a year at that point, and several operations later with broken legs and so forth, I'm still paying dues. Everybody has a strike against them, very few are handed a silver platter. Some are, but even they have other things that get into the diagram.

I think it made me the clichéd Type A hard worker, overachiever, all the normal descriptions of somebody that's pushing ahead. I'm pretty cool with pain and operating. I would have been a very good doctor, I wouldn't have a problem with that, because when you're a kid and you go through it yourself – "Oh, you're a great patient, Dave. Here's a gold star and an ice cream soda" – it does mold your personality. But of course there were times during the teenage years when you're not playing ball, you're not doing anything. The music, thank God I found the music because that was obviously a way for me forming my own personality away from the so-called mainstream, especially in the '50s and '60s.

Things that happen in life, especially if they're down things, things that don't appear to be positive, definitely build that greater feeling for humanity. I don't know if you express it by being a lawyer or a bus driver or an artist, but I think it comes into the equation somewhere. Empathy of course, because you know what it is to be down. I think being a kid, it just becomes part of your soul.

CHARLES JAFFE: When I was sixteen, my junior year of high school, I had something called Guillain-Barré Syndrome, which is likely an autoimmune response in the nervous system. It's like polio except that it affects sensory as well as motor function. I was in an iron lung for a while, and it taught me a lot about never forgetting the fragility of being alive and the necessity of pulling on all those things that are essentially human. It made me conversant with people who are depressed or ill or suicidal, because that sort of near death experience did make me feel deeply moved.

At the time, I was sixteen years old. The Beatles were coming to town, and my memory of it was I was listening to a lot of Beatles on the radio. Then I just wanted to get better and get the hell out of there, and I had no concept at the time that I was as ill as I was. I learned all of that afterwards, but I had some post-traumatic anxiety effects from that. I still don't like to be under water or be in enclosed places too much. There's some of that, but I think that the long-term effect of that really was to give me a sense of we're all going to be asleep for a really long time, so while we're here it's worth being awake and alert and active and loving and involved as much as possible.

DAVID BLOOM: Did your soul change when you reached adulthood?

TED COHEN: When I graduated from high school, I tried going to the University of Illinois, and it didn't work very well. I was a really bad student. Then I got kind of depressed and anxious, so I ran away from home and went to New York for a few months. I took a few lessons there on how to play the drums from Cozy Cole's Drum School, and I found these odd jobs. I worked for some legal reporting firm. I worked for something called the Frackville Pajama Company, so I could go to work every day in the Empire State Building. I just was amazed by the city. I ran around, listened to music. Then I came back and came to the University of Chicago, and it worked better. It was not a very sensible choice. It just worked out well.

One feature that saved my life I didn't know about when I came, it's not like this anymore - it hasn't been for many years - but when I came here almost every class you took lasted all year. The whole grade was based on one big exam at the end. Exam would last six hours. I was really screwing around. I was an apprentice beatnik, so I was often out of the city. I did a lot of hitchhiking. I didn't go to class. I wasn't even in town. I'd be on the North Side listening to poetry readings and trying to hear jazz in various places. If I'd been in a regular school with regular classes, I would have flunked because I wasn't showing up. If you showed up in May and were able to read the stuff and pass, that was good. That's not why I came. It just turned out to be a lucky result.

PATTI VASQUEZ: When I was a kid I played Little League baseball for five years on an all-boys' team. It was obvious that they didn't want me there. I was a tomboy. I didn't grow up thinking I was pretty. My mom would always tell me, "You're more exotic than the other girls," because I was in an all-white grade school and I was a Latina. So I never thought of myself as a typical pretty girl. When I started doing comedy and people started saying, "You're too pretty to be a comic," that kind of fell hard on my ears. Maybe that is why I make so many faces. But I've always made faces. I've always been kind of a goofball.

Sometimes I have that feeling when I take the stage that "Oh, what she's going to say? This is all going to be complaining about being a woman, complaining about men." That's some women's style. There are a lot of men out there who complain about women, who are very misogynist, and somehow that's okay. But if a woman is on stage complaining about guys, that makes her a man hater. That gets tiring. I've been told before, "I almost didn't come to see your show because I don't like female comics." Or, "No offense, I don't usually like female comics, but you were funny." I try to accept that.

Years ago I used to get mad. There are so few female comics out there that if you see one bad female comic, that's probably the one you'll remember. There are a lot of bad comics out there. It's just possible that the women are easier to remember. But now when people tell me that, I just take it the best way I can. I like what I do. I don't care what everybody says.

SOUL SOURCES

The most powerful weapon on Earth is the human soul on fire.
-Ferdinand Foch

DAVID BLOOM: Can you tell me who has made the biggest impact on your soul or soulfulness?

TED COHEN: My wife. She has a quicker and more reliable sense of how other people are feeling than I have. I've actually written a fair amount of stuff about the moral need to be able – at least in your imagination – to understand how other people feel. I'm a big fan of the ability to do that. I think without that ability we're lost, but it isn't as readily awakened in me as it is in my wife. I read about people whom I don't know personally, but I'm convinced there are people like this. Certain Catholic priests do certain things with their lives. There are people, in a way, who go too far. You can be so upset and debilitated by all the shit that happens to people in the world that you can barely live in the world.

BOB WILLEMS: There is a priest, actually, who had a huge influence on me as a kid in grade school. Priests to a kid in grade school can seem nonhuman; they're a figure more than they are a person. This particular priest was a very human person and very open about why he chose to do what he was doing with his life. I'm sure he gets more kids to think critically about what are the values in life, what your life's work is going to be all about, and the priesthood.

He'd spend hours every day on Fridays just visiting people who are elderly and shut in or ill, terminally ill in some cases. He was about influencing people's lives in a very profound way, and he knew that that meant every Friday he was going to go see Sally, who was eighty-five years old and didn't leave her house and she had nobody to talk to, and so she was going to talk about everything that was going on with her life. He knew that was part of the bargain when he decided to make that decision on what he was going to do with his life.

I wasn't in the age where I questioned Catholicism or organized religion or the institution of the Church or any of those things. To me it was kind of just one big ball of wax. But later I started questioning what is Catholicism, what is the organized Church, what role do those things play in society and how much do I want to be a part of that, and how much do I want to pursue spirituality in a different way.

I never lost touch with him, and I don't think, even if he met me today and knew that I'm the guy who's not in church every Sunday and I'm not the guy who's considering priesthood anymore, I'm sure he would feel that his lasting impact on me works on a much more fundamental level of like, "I'm a human being, I have these values, and I have this vision for what life can be like or what my life can be like, and I want to share this with you." He touched my soul.

STUDS TERKEL: Both my brothers played a role, in two different ways, and I suppose I'm part of both. My oldest brother was the reader of books and he taught me a lot of that. My other brother loved life and he loved dancing, kind of pop music, you know; so both affected me. But oh, books – Mark Twain. When I read *Huckleberry Finn* I liked it, but when I first read it I was only twelve or thirteen and I didn't understand all of the implications. Well, later on when I was nineteen, twenty years old, I loved *Look Homeward Angel* by Thomas Wolfe. There was associating: his mother was a tough little sparrow, my mother was a tough little sparrow. His mother ran a boarding house, my mother ran a rooming house and hotel. I had a brother named Ben; he had a brother named Ben. Then there was *Studs Lonigan*. I betcha that did it. Studs Lonigan, that's how I got the nickname, 'cause I liked that trilogy so much.

TOM BURRELL: I consider my mother to be soulful in the sense she is not afraid to be expressive. She is not afraid to take chances, just in the way that she has been able to express to me, and to my sister, things about life without the benefit of any kind of extensive learning. Just the idea that she was able to let me be me, I think that is a kind of an indication of that.

What she basically did, which some people might even think of as not being as responsible as a parent ought to be, is she always gave me the impression that I was intelligent and that I was able to think for myself. Not only that, but when I wanted to do something, she had a very skillful way of allowing me to think it through and to do it. What she and my grandmother would always say is "Just let Junior go out and try stuff," (that's what they called me), "let Junior go out and try stuff and if he finds out that it is not a thing to do then he will stop. Setting pins at the bowling alley until three o'clock in the morning? Well, he's there, we know he's there. If he gets tired he'll stop. Taking those Charles Atlas correspondence courses, okay, he'll do that and then he'll stop and do something else."

She also had a great skill at facilitating my thinking things through and quietly encouraging it. You know, "Oh, is that what you want to do?" Now in her head she's probably thinking that's the stupidest thing, but she would say, "Is that what you want to do? Did you think about how it's going to work, how you're going to do it?" And of course, sometimes in the questioning I would go back and say, "Um hmm, maybe I shouldn't be doing this at all." She never told me not to, but she caused me to ask questions about it to myself, so I would think, okay maybe I should rethink that.

DAVID BLOOM: You told me your mom was a very soulful person. What about your dad?

PATTI VASQUEZ: Absolutely. I think he was religious. I don't think he would say he was soulful. My dad loved to go out and talk to people and to make them laugh no matter where they were. If they're in an elevator, if they're at Dunkin' Donuts, if they're in his cab when he was driving, he loved to touch other people and to talk to them and see what was going on in their lives. I think my mom is soulful, too. My mom is much more quiet but she is extremely soulful. She's always finding herself through art, through reading, through all kinds of different experiences.

TED COHEN: The town doctor was a Czech immigrant who I never completely understood but I wanted very much to please. He seemed like a substantial person to me. My grandfather, whom I didn't understand very well, was also an immigrant. I made the same mistake of lots of people in my generation. I got real interested in where these guys came from and what they did, why they did it, how they did it, and the terrific odds they battled against in order to do it. I got interested in all of it a little too late – like around the time they died. I've got millions of questions that I no longer have anybody to get answers from. It's too bad.

The past is a weight, and it's good to be free of it, but on the other hand there are things you could get and you don't. I'd like very much to know how my grandfather came to settle in a little town and open a general store. How Jews and Catholics who don't usually get along somehow got along in that town, because the Ku Klux Klan was a pain in the ass to both of them. I learned all of that too late to really ask them about it.

DAVID BLOOM: How do you know, at first sight, if someone is soulful?

BARRETT DOSS: I think when you meet someone and you see that they're a very happy person, they're happy with who they are. Maybe not in their situation, but you can see that they do have shadows of happiness. You can see it in their eyes, or you can see it in their aura, for lack of a better word. You can sense it from people. At least I can, so if someone actually seems like they're a genuinely happy person, or they're really excited about something, that's where I can see soul.

ZACK GRAHAM: Yes, I think you can tell when you meet someone that has soul. You can tell, and it's not a surface feeling at all. It's something that when you shake their hand or when you look at them in the eyes, you know that they are about something, as opposed to just trying to get by, trying to do this, trying to do that. They really have soul. They really have a conscious.

They really have a core. They really know themselves. If you look someone in the eyes, and they've got that soul, you know it. They know it, and everybody else knows it.

BILL KURTIS: Ray Krone was on death row for about four and a half years, spent ten years in a penitentiary as an innocent person, his living condition twenty-three and a half hours a day in a cell alone, isolated from other human beings, lacking in interaction with another person even to shake hands, and ultimately released because of DNA. He felt it was terrible punishment, much worse than an execution. But he said he learned that if he could make it within the space of that small room the size of broom closet, he could make it anywhere. And he became stronger for the experience. It forces you to discover yourself and your soul, because all you have to do is think about it. And so he went inside; that's how you do time in prison: You go inside and you can go anywhere you want, mentally.

ZACK GRAHAM: I've met people who I thought were an influence to my soul and weren't. I've met people who I didn't think, and were. I met people that I knew, and it's just amazing. Sometimes you see someone, and they've devoted their life to something, or they've taught you something, or they see something in you. You really admire that person, and you really think highly about that person. What have people taught me? My dad is the first and foremost. He is my center. When I'm worried, when I'm confused, whatever I'm going through, he's there. He teaches me so much every day. It's amazing.

OSCAR BROWN, JR.: Of course my parents were a strong influence. My aunts and uncles, we had a close family. Beyond that, the teachers and the preachers and the authority figures that I came in contact with as a young person. There were no writers as such at that point in my immediate circle. Reading certain literature, I liked Howard Fast or Richard Wright. Then I began to read poetry. Some of it was enforced like Shakespeare, but I enjoyed Shakespeare. I read Keats and Shelley. Then I was reading Countee Cullen and Langston Hughes. I was influenced by that as far as writing was concerned.

When I was in college, I went to the University of Wisconsin, and I flunked everything except English Composition. I made A-plus in English Composition, because I discovered that I could write. If they asked for a one hundred word theme in our little theme books, I could write a hundred word poem. This just dazzled my teacher. That was the only one I dazzled. The rest of it like English grammar and all that stuff, Spanish, I took that at one point. All of that I flunked out, because I just didn't go to class.

Reading is the main thing I got out of my whole education, learning to read English, and the Dewey Decimal System. If you had that, you can find out anything you want to find out. Just go to the library and look it up. I got stuff out of the streets, out of listening, out of just growing up, out of participating in life as I grew up. I had heroes: Paul Robeson, Dick Durham. As I began to appreciate entertainers, I was a fan of this one or that one. I loved Josh White, for example, Robeson again, Marian Anderson. I had quite an eclectic taste.

Robeson was sort of a mythic figure in my household as I was coming up. He was doing movies, and he was a great concert singer. Gradually he began to become a political figure. That emerged particularly after World War II. The progressive movement, the Progressive Party began to emerge, and I was coming into manhood at that point and becoming politically aware. I ultimately joined the Communist Party when I was about twenty years old and ran for political office.

The first time I voted, I voted for me. That was in 1948, and Robeson came to a church at 55th and Indiana. Down in the basement we had a little youth rally, and he made a speech on my behalf and explained the universality of music to our audience, the common character of different languages, how people from China and Africa use intonation to change the meaning of what they were saying. He could illustrate that, because he was a renowned linguist. That was a very memorable thing.

I have to include among those who influenced me: Martin Luther King, Malcolm X, Joe Lewis, and President Roosevelt. A whole bunch of people at all levels of activity. When there is a spirit around everybody, there's a spirit of each of us as individuals, and that will remain with all the people who ever encountered you. In another sense, it extends beyond them to everybody they encounter, because we are a part of… What is it? Every man is a piece of the continent. We are all involved in the same thing: "Never sending for whom the bell tolls."

CLIFF COLNOT: When I got to Florida State as a freshman, I had the privilege of meeting one of the music professors who was a jazz trumpet player, and he became my mentor for the four years that I was at Florida State, and I learned a great deal about humanity and a great deal about teaching and music and education from him. Dr. Madsen was soulful in all contexts to everyone that he interacted with.

ANDREA COSNOWSKY: The first person that jumps out at me, because I'm a big fan, is B.B. King. Here's a man who's eighty years old, and he's been through a lot in his life. He has remained steadfast, and success hasn't changed him, diabetes hasn't changed him. He is just who he is from the get-go. I think as a person he's changed from the time he was twenty to the time he's eighty, but musically he's always been who he is. That sense of integrity is admirable to me.

BOB WILLEMS: Ten years ago, I had an opportunity to hear Cesar Chavez speak at a meeting in one of these organizations that I work with. This guy was electrifying. He was in front of a group of three hundred people, never met any of those people before. We're not like farm workers, we are not union people. We were people who worked on environmental advocacy campaigns. This guy walked into this room and there was like an instantaneous bond.

These groups were nerdy recent college graduates who were chanting "Cesar Chavez" in Spanish. You felt this kind of brotherhood and this connection with him. It was about putting that seed into the individual's head that you are not alone in this. Not only that you are not alone, but you and all these other people here together, or in a society there, are people. You can act as a people and you can determine what you want to be as a people and how you want things to be. The best leaders inspire that kind of thinking. They make it seem easy to come together and do stuff together. Together we are people.

TOM BURRELL: I think that the way that soulful people behave is that they behave more independently. They are more introspective. They can be more demonstrative and less defensive. Conversely, people who lack soul are people who tend to be more restrained, more conservative, more inhibited, sometimes less expressive. I think a person who is soulful is more likely to be vulnerable, to feel free to express not only thoughts and ideas, but feelings.

ERWIN DRECHSLER: A lot has to do with the world that my parents created for me. They were both Holocaust survivors. It wasn't something that was talked about a lot in the house but it was recognized. I think because of their experience and what they went through, the most important thing to them was 'now,' that they were here, they were alive, and they had a family. It's something that was communicated to me through their actions, through their dialogues, through the kind of activities that we did around the house. It wasn't about worrying what was going to happen. It wasn't about talking what had happened. It was to enjoy the moment and be thankful for it and embrace it.

David Taffet

THE SOUL AND DEATH

*Nobody grows old merely by living a number of years.
We grow old by deserting our ideals. Years may wrinkle the skin,
but to give up enthusiasm wrinkles the soul.*

-Samuel Ullman

STUDS TERKEL: A little girl next door died of Scarlet Fever. They used to put up signs in those days: "Scarlet Fever, contagious." And the little girl – I was about eight, she was about eight – she died, and that's when my brother was telling me about someday… And I said, "Pop too?" and my father, he said yeah. And that was a big one for me. It was something heavy on my little chest. And that was something: the awareness that this life is going to end, even for those most dear to you. You hardly thought of yourself because you're too young to do that, but someone close to you, you see. And then when he died in the '50s, that was the most traumatic moment of my life.

CHARLES JAFFE: When I was twenty-four my dad died. He had just turned sixty, and he had stomach cancer. He was very, very ill, and he was dying at home. We used to gather in my parent's bedroom. My parents always shared a double bed, and they were hanging out in bed together. My father said to my mother, "I don't know how you can stand to be near me. I'm like a stick figure. I look like I just got out of the concentration camp." And she said to him, "You're my husband, and none of that matters. We're just here." It was a very, very moving moment to capture the goodness and the richness of human expression at its best. Unafraid, unashamed, reaching way, way in and overcoming all kinds of fears. It was soulfulness in its highest level, I think.

JEWEL TANCY: When my parents died I lost convenience. I lost dependability. I lost major figures that molded me and made me who I am as a person. I lost knowing that I could pick up the phone and go, "Hey, Mom." I lost knowing that the doorbell would be ringing and it would be Dad saying, "Hey, how are you doing, kiddo? You're working on music today? Are you writing new songs? When are you going to be singing that?" The support, knowledge, I lost that. But I gained growth. I gained new lessons in my life. I gained, learning that everything that's here is here but it's not here. I gained self-knowledge. That's what I gained. That's a continual learning process.

VAN SANDWICK: My soul, if I were to die, will get carried on. I would want it to be good, nurture it throughout my life and make sure I treat people well and do good things and nourish my soul. If it were to go on and eventually go to somebody else, it will be a good soul for them to start with.

DON MEADE: The soul is you. Everybody has one. So it exists; it's in the marrow of our bones. How we manifest it, make its mechanics work, determines our success or our failure, or our being what we are. When we die, new ones come into the world. It's a matter of trading old souls for a new life. Okay? So it's evolutionary, it keeps evolving, it keeps going. Day One, the day you come into the world, you begin to die; you spend the rest of your life dying. I believe this.

ELSA MORA: Some people when they go, they have to die, because they committed the crime, and they go to the death penalty. In the last minutes, they have "renacimiento." We say they are born again. It's too late, unfortunately, but there is always a little door there that you can open even if it's in the last minute. I say this because I really trust in human nature. I think that the good part of human nature is always there in every person, in every single person. That's why I never think there are bad kids or good kids or bad adults, no. There is always a big rainbow of everything.

JEWEL TANCY: Life and death are so powerful. Those are things that we really can't see. Life, we can see. And definitely when we go to a funeral, we see the person lying in the casket. For me that was very soulful because I realize that, okay, Mom isn't here, Dad isn't here. I can't get to these people anymore. They're gone because their soul is gone. They don't have shadows anymore.

SOUL EXPRESSIONS

Gabby Orcutt

We reveal our souls in professions and pastimes, from the arts to commercial pursuits. Certainly, soulfulness is the bedrock of worthwhile music – whether it's jazz, classical or pop. Music means very little if it doesn't display deep feelings.

Soul music – as we know it today – emerged from gospel, the African-American church, and major record labels of the 1950s and '60s, but soulful music also exists in other eras and cultures. Today we question whether soul persists in contemporary musical forms.

The visual arts can also exhibit soul, as can literature (including songwriting), dance, comedy, TV, radio, and film. Even carpenters and ironworkers, any caring craftspeople, pour their souls into their work. Any job will be soulful if it requires high levels of emotional involvement.

In this chapter, participants discuss their vocations and avocations – whether in music, the pulpit, academia, business or food preparation – and how they bring their soulfulness into what might easily be just another way to earn a paycheck. Even in the courtroom, justice is best served with a substantial helping of soul.

Stan Getz

SOUL IN MUSIC

Music is a moral law. It gives soul to the universe, wings to the mind, flight to the imagination, and charm and gaiety to life and to everything.

-Plato

OSCAR BROWN, JR.: No other species of life has anything remotely like music. I'm not talking about bird calls or whales making their sounds. I'm talking about where you set up a rhythm, set up harmonies. Where you have a melodic idea, theme, where you might add lyrics. Trees don't do that. It doesn't interest birds. They don't fly by and say "Hey, let's check out the concert." They're oblivious to that.

Whatever soul is, it is carried on music in a way that's unique to us as a species. If we want it to lead towards something that we believe prospers the human race, then we've got to communicate this spirit in the best way, and that's music.

TOM BURRELL: What soul meant to me about music was that it was raw, unstudied, unvarnished, gutsy, unrefined, true, a real sincere expression of emotions, and that it's done in an artful way. I felt that the artfulness came out of the sincerity of it. It wasn't like I am going to purposely work on being artful here, it's like hey, I have this art thing I want to express, and that emotional thing elicits an emotional response.

STUDS TERKEL: Music that's good, no matter what form it takes, is soulful. Are you moved when you hear a string quartet? Sure. How about the choral group from Beethoven's Ninth toward the end? They don't call those soul singers. But of course they are.

DAVE LIEBMAN: Soul means having to do with the feeling beyond the notes, beyond the technique, beyond the knowledge. Usually when I teach, well, we know the trilogy is mind, body and spirit. This is just old stuff and I, for the sake of ease, call it head, hand and heart. Heart meaning the feeling and what it is that really comes out of the work for the listener, for the viewer, or for the reader, depending on the art.

TED COHEN: There is no other art that has the developed technical vocabulary that music has. Books like I've got lying around here like the Harvard Dictionary, the Music Grove Dictionary. You can just find term after term, but this technical vocabulary has grown up partly in response to the fact that in ordinary language it's almost impossible to talk about language. There's nothing to say. You just listen and you get it, or you don't. It's not to say you can't be helped. You can learn a little. It helps a lot in music like it does in basketball to learn how to play a little. It gives you a little insight into what's happening when we hear people play.

OSCAR BROWN, JR.: Music didn't start out with soulful qualities. That which we consider soulful, as far as music is concerned, I think, has to conform to Duke Ellington's dictum: "It don't mean a thing if it ain't got that swing." That's basically what we're talking about in soulful music.

Duke Ellington

JAZZ

Jazz music is an aural souvenir of mankind's attempt to express the intangible – the heart, the soul – through art.

-Maxwell Chandler

RICK KOGAN: I do this radio show. And one of my arguments on this show, when I play a certain kind of music… And my tastes are absolutely eclectic. I'll hear something and I'll like it and I'll say, "Gee, I never thought I liked country." My argument is, to the listeners: I'll play you a song. It's four minutes long. It is a jazz tune. You may be one of these people who spend fifty years saying, "I don't like jazz," for reasons that are your business, not mine. Or, "I don't like rock," or, "I don't like country music." I say, "I'm going to play this. Give it four minutes. If you don't like this, then you're totally justified in saying, for the rest of your life, 'I don't like jazz.'" I'd prefer if you said, "I don't like the jazz that Rick Kogan plays on his show." You're justified, for me, in saying you don't like jazz. But think about it: What if you do like it?

People involve themselves with the superficiality of jazz without digging for its soul.

-Stan Getz

DON MEADE: Universally, America knows less about this art form, jazz, which is the only indigenous art form, than any other society or culture in the world. And that's probably the saddest thing of all my seventy-five years. So many of us had to leave this country and go elsewhere to get any recognition. I've lived to see churches denounce this music. They said it had nothing to do with the soul. It was devil's music. Yet in those twelve notes, there's nothing there except truth.

DAVID BLOOM: So much of art – and jazz, in particular – has to do with conveying deep feeling. That's the way I look at it. There are all kinds of jazz players with virtuosic technique who can buzz around on their instruments, but they might not be saying much or might not be providing a very deep emotional experience.

TED COHEN: Given what I think soul means, I agree with you. Stuff is supposed to, if not directly convey feelings, at least somehow get across how the artist feels. The whole idea is you've got to be compassionate without being sappy. That's the deal. That's hard, because you can be so worried about being sappy that you don't respond at all. You're just going to have a stiff upper lip. You can make the mistake of thinking that someone who doesn't express his feelings the way you do isn't expressing them at all. It may just be that you don't understand his language.

CHARLES JAFFE: There can be a deep sharing of an essence without words at all. And a deep sense of inner understanding that has nothing to do with words. A great example of that is playing music where the level of communication and the level of exposure and the level of that combination of personal exploration, in the company of others and in a synergistic way with others, can go beyond words.

JEWEL TANCY: You can be moved by something and not necessarily understand it, but you can still have that experience. It's okay if you don't quite understand everything. But there's something about feeling. There's something about the emotion. There's something about being moved. It has to be back to this whole concept of soul. It has to be moving constantly.

BLANCHE MANNING: Sometimes if I'm feeling down and out, I might go and get my horn and start playing the blues or playing really soulful as best I can. It's a glorious feeling to me. I could play saxophone all day long. Frankly, that's one of the most important facets of my life, music, and specifically playing the saxophone. I really get this wonderful feeling when it appears that people are enjoying what I'm playing.

DAVE LIEBMAN: I lived the dream and I'll never take it for granted. I was very lucky. The one thing that I got most of all is: When you get on the stage, this is business. This is not fun and games. The first priority is the music and it can only be an hour. You got to be there a hundred and fifteen percent, because those other guys are a hundred and fifteen percent. That's something you don't get from the book, you can't get it from listening, you can't even get it from three feet away. You can only get it when you are on the stage standing next to somebody, playing.

DAVID BLOOM: How do you feel about someone like the legendary saxophone player, Gene Ammons? What sort of effect does he have on listeners and how is that different from other musicians, vis-à-vis soul?

DON MEADE: Well, Gene Ammons came up in a soulful era, where people listened, and they found themselves in that music. It related to them. It was about sorrows, about happiness, about the weekend and hard times. Everybody played each other's music. They don't do that today. No indictment, but I know some young ones that walk up onstage and don't even say good evening, sit down and proceed to play their music. There's no camaraderie, no family up on stage. If you go back to that bebop era that broke from the big bands and formed sextets, octets, any of the smaller groups, there was camaraderie, talking up onstage. If you noticed Monk when he was playing, he decided to take that coat off, never did take that hat off, but he'd dance, go around the piano, go over and start talking to Ben Riley or whoever was on drums, Ed Blackwell, any of them.

Dizzy used to do things up onstage and he'd be hollering at the piano player over there. Exchange going on. Give and take. This is what it's about. There's the manifestation of the soul working at its best, on all cylinders. But the bottom line is the blues. Bottom line is gospel. Eight over twelve, twelve over eight, the basic eight. You know, jazz grew out of that, because that's how you got the sixteenth note. Boom chick-a-boom-chick-a-boom. Ding ding ding. But we can't forget from where we came.

James Brown

SOUL MUSIC OF THE 1950s AND '60s

Soul is when you take a song and make it a part of you – a part that's so true, so real, people think it must have happened to you. It's like electricity – we don't really know what it is, but it's a force that can light a room.

-Ray Charles

CLIFF COLNOT: In the late 1950s in the black jazz community, there was a movement of soul jazz. I found it very interesting to relate that nascent movement with what occurred in the early 1960s, the soul music movement, the pop rhythm and blues soul music movement, because the soul jazz movement was based primarily on the notion that we could turn a negative reality, in other words the black experience in America, into an empowering, powerful, positive experience. I believe that the archetypal soul music movement picked up on the notion that soul was not some pejorative notion that white people would parody and ridicule but in fact was a mechanism by which to galvanize black pride and empowerment.

OSCAR BROWN, JR.: What we're talking about was generally out of the black church, the Southern Baptist or Pentecostal churches primarily, out of the work songs and the blues and the secular music that was created and played by people who were experiencing slavery and what came after that. When we reached a certain political development in which we said we are equal to others – we must have equal rights, we must have liberation – we began to reach back into what we were and to bring that forward in all its aspects, particularly in music.

CLIFF COLNOT: I think the term soul music developed out of an intergenerational, interracial, and interregional phenomenon in the South. I would say that the most soulful period during my lifetime was between 1959 and 1967 when Otis Redding died. It didn't end in a bang, but I think it petered out over that year or so, from 1967 to 1968.

Otis Redding was successful in breaking down racial and cultural and economic barriers vis-à-vis his music. I remember reading his remarks about how he was able to get drugged rock and rollers, white-bread suburbanites, older folks, younger folks of all stripes to be moved by his music. In that sense, I think that period, that decade in the 1960s, created the momentum that allowed an entire country to see firsthand – and even experience – soulfulness.

There's a certain amount of historical fact that relates to the notion that at the end of the 1960s the black music community and the black business community turned on the white producers and musicians. There was a watershed moment at a convention of black deejays in which there was this groundswell of resentment against the white establishment that had orchestrated, in large part, the soul music tradition for ten years.

With this radical shift, this divisiveness in the community, the creation of the music was no longer soulful. The minute the black record community and/or deejays, the black entrepreneurs, the black publishers, etcetera felt as if they were being ripped off by their collaborators, it doesn't seem to me inexplicable why that would be the end of the music. The music was based on mutual trust, mutual collaboration, egalitarian values. When those changed, which they did in the late 1960s, then it was over.

I think at that point the future, the next thirty-five years, was a harbinger of what followed from 1968. In other words, it's fascinating to consider these cultural and sociological and political anomalies that were directly related to this community of blacks, whites, Jews, men, women who created this aesthetic, this music called soul music which lasted ten years. Basically, in my opinion, in the last thirty years the institutionalized racism and classism that preceded that decade have come back in spades.

If your question is, is there any residue of that in this new millennium? I don't see it. I think it left America in the same way that a shooting star does, in a burst, and we never saw it again to speak of. Of course, that's extreme rhetoric. There always were, and there always will be, pockets of soulfulness, but if you're asking me on the macro level, "Is there any residue from that decade? Is Otis Redding's legacy still observable in a significant way in American culture?" I would say no.

OSCAR BROWN, JR.: During the 1960s, you had Peter, Paul & Mary and Bob Dylan and The Temptations. Everybody. "War. What is it good for? Absolutely nothing. Say it again." You had Aretha Franklin talking about "Respect," "Think." You had all kinds of this going into the culture. Control of the music business was seized by corporate interests that want to drown all of that out and take that quality away from music. The music industry is run by people who hate musicians. Don't want to pay them. Never contribute anything to the development of new music. Simply want to clone stuff that they can replace. All they hear is the ring of the cash register. That's the music to their ears. That's like the treasure falling into the hands of the forty thieves.

STUDS TERKEL: I think that gospel music today has been commercialized too. There's no question. By the way, gospel and spiritual are different eras, epochs in African-American society. The music of slavery was spirituals, aside from the work songs, and they called upon the Old Testament to the New: "Did my Lord deliver Daniel, then why not every man?," "Joshua fit the battle of Jericho." These are Old Testament references. "Swing Low Sweet Chariot," "Crossing the River Jordan." Well, the River Jordan in reality was that swamp land separating free country from slave country, you see, so it had meaning. They were code words. Those were spirituals. But post-Civil War, long after, you might say Northern music became gospel music, or good news music, and a lot of the gospel music is commercial, very commercial indeed.

The Staple Singers with Booker T and the MGs

SOUL BROTHERS

Music fills the infinite between two souls.

-Rabindranath Tagore

TED COHEN: One of the oldest clichés about art is that it gives you experiences that you don't get otherwise. You can get some sense of what it is to have the blues even if you don't have them. You didn't grow up as the descendent of slaves, downtrodden and so forth. Still, when Billie Holiday sings, it comes through to you. You can understand it, and you might even be able to learn to sing that way.

Everybody makes fun. Some white guy who was born in an upper middle-class suburb starts singing chain gang songs. It sounds really inauthentic. There's something really weird about that, but the possibility is there.

STUDS TERKEL: The word soul is very often associated with black music. Soul brother: "He's my soul brother" one black guy says to another, or white guys; white guys do it. Half the words in the entertainment world are Jewish, the other half are black. Even the gestures, the handshake and everything else. So here two minorities, you see, have altered and enriched our very vocabulary. And there you have it. I think we got it. Make of it what you will.

OSCAR BROWN, JR.: Robeson pointed out how oppressed peoples tended to sing minor keys. He could sing some stuff from the kibbutz in Israel – I guess it was Israel at that time – but anyway he could sing from that culture. He could sing from the Welsh coal miners, and he could do the blues, the gospel from here. There was this minor tone that seemed to reflect what the people were feeling in different cultures, different soul but the same thing.

TED COHEN: This is a mistake to think that if you don't have this experience, you can't imagine it. That's what art's about, right? Look what jazz did. The French got it, for goodness sake. The Italians, the English, this stuff works all over the world. People whose history and experience couldn't be more different from that of the American black community, namely Scandinavians, have become some of the greatest jazz connoisseurs and performers in the world. Now how can that be? The answer is: because they have the imagination to understand the music.

This music would be dead if it weren't for white audiences. Black people in the audience, there will be some, but they will be older. The rest of the audience will be white, and there will be some young white people. Is this inauthentic? No, it's not inauthentic. Why has the black audience turned away? That's a good question. Maybe they did it because they don't want to like the same thing that white people like. That's a shame. It costs them something.

Luciano Pavarotti

SOUL OR NOT?

Of the three prerequisites of genius; the first is soul, the second is soul, and the third is soul.

-Edwin P. Whipple

DAVID BLOOM: With all the music you've heard, was there one particularly soulful performance that you recall?

DON MEADE: Ben Webster was up in Gothamburg one night. He was probably at the top of his form. And he suddenly started crying. Everybody thought, "Oh, jeez, what's wrong with the old man, is he sick? What's going to happen?" So they waited until it was over with, and they went up and said, "Ben are you all right?" And he said, "Yeah, I played so well, I had to cry myself." That's soul. That's soul. Knowing where you are, knowing that pitch, that level, that pendulum, that that extra mile is just a breath away. From it all being exactly right. That's the workings of the soul.

BILL HORBERG: I've always associated soulfulness with what is authentic about the human condition, about the human voice, about the way we connect and communicate with each other. As a young boy growing up in the streets of Chicago, I would say my first encounter with what I felt was the sincere, soulful expression of the human interior was probably at the Maxwell Street market. I used to go down there with friends, with my older sister. We'd see these amazing street performances of guys that had clearly lived the life.

Another thing that leaps out of me is maybe as a twelve or thirteen-year-old getting out at night with a friend of mine, sneaking out from the parents, going into some blues bar and getting really up close in the front row with a guy named Big Walter Horton who was out there playing the harmonica. On the high end of the spectrum of the notes of life, there was just something about this gangly, tall, drunk, beautiful and just deeply, deeply expressive and musical dude, who was right up in our face blowing the harmonica. It just washed over me. I said, "Wow, I want to play the harmonica. I want to have a life in which I feel connected to those kinds of moments and experiences."

DON MEADE: A Baptist choir on Sunday morning, how it can propel itself, how it can crank itself up. Many souls are working. It works because nobody's talking, everybody's singing. We all can sing together, but we all can't talk together; somebody's gotta listen while the other one talks. We have to let it be. If we let the soul wander, like the soul does – this is a personal belief – it's everywhere, and what we do at that time and in that place plays the greater role.

DAVID BLOOM: There's a lot of soulful music out there. What's soulful to you?

TOM BREWER: Before I actually sat down and thought about it, I just thought of being soulful as being like James Brown or something.

DEREK CHIAMPAS: That's what I thought. Like soul food or soul power.

CHRISSY DELACOTTA: I think why they say "soul" music and "soul" food is because it makes your soul feel good. Comforting.

NATHAN WORCESTER: I think soulful music isn't something that makes you feel good. Well, it does in a way, but if someone is putting a lot of effort into what they're doing and they just send out a good vibe, it will send a message to you: "Wow, this person's really trying their best."

PHILLIP VERNA: I was thinking of the Tom Waits' album, his new one. It's kind of depressing and moving. I think generally soul and music has a lot to do with lyrics and how they're projected, as opposed to how they're played.

JON SWANK: When I listen to the Doors, Jim Morrison's lyrics, he's not even trying to hide his feelings. He's kind of given up hope for the world. He's just expressing himself soulfully.

CHRISTIAN STEINBARTH: The new Johnny Cash CD really moves me because it kind of sounds like he's dying throughout the entire album, and it's really sad.

VAN SANDWICK: Whenever I listen to Stevie Ray Vaughan, it's like he's telling a story through his guitar. It makes me feel really good and really bad at the same time because I can't play it.

ANN SAWYER: For some reason, the Van Morrison album "Astral Weeks," I just like it.

VAN SANDWICK: I think in all honesty, Beethoven's Moonlight Sonata, the third movement. I like a lot of songs and a lot of music, but that one just – you just feel it. Other songs will be like, "Yeah this is cool. I feel this." But that one you're just like, "Whoa." It sends a message to you.

RICK KOGAN: There are some people who have been vilified, like Eminem. He's an interesting example to me. Is this a soulful person? Listen to his music. Is this guy sharing something real about himself? Listen to the song "Cleaning Out My Closet," which is about his relationship with his mother. This man is sharing something that is absolutely genuine. I am not the target Eminem audience or the Eminem fan. I love this kid. I love this kid. I get a look, I get a glimpse of his soul. Can I share it in any way other than listening to his music – and buying his music? No. But I am sharing it. I am responding to him.

Now there are people who think that "Britney Spears, man, the way she sings, she's got soul!" Well, I haven't seen or felt any, so I'm not diminishing what some kid feels about her, but I would argue with that kid, because it's all too pre-packaged, to my mind.

TED COHEN: Anybody who uses the word soul would know what someone meant who said that one big difference between Ella Fitzgerald and Billie Holiday is Billie Holiday's got soul in a way that Ella doesn't. Does it mean that Billie Holiday's a better singer? I don't think so. You think that there's more emotion that comes through when Billie Holiday sings than when Ella Fitzgerald sings? I don't think so. I read once somebody said that when Ella sings a line like "My man's left me," it sounds like she's just going to the corner to buy some bread. Ella's not the best person to sing the blues, but Billie Holiday is not the best person to sing scat. It's another kind of music.

Ray Charles has got soul in a way that Frank Sinatra doesn't. Does it mean that Ray's a better singer? I don't think so. It's a different thing, a different way of doing things. Soul's a real good thing, but I just don't think it's the only thing. Frank Sinatra is a terrific singer, but there would be no more point in having Frank sing the blues than playing Beethoven's Fifth Symphony on the xylophone.

BILL KURTIS: I heard a Hawaiian man named Iz, who weighs about three hundred and fifty pounds, play a tiny little ukulele and sing "Over the Rainbow," then morph into "It's a Beautiful World," you know, the Louie Armstrong. And I came to tears – because he sang it like I had never heard it before.

RICK KOGAN: You'll see instances of soulfulness in music and art, and that's where everybody seems to say, "Well, that's real soul." Lou Rawls had soul, Al Green had soul, Billie Holiday had soul, John Coltrane had soul. You're not going to get an argument from anybody. But what that implies is that in order to have soul, it's incumbent on having transcendent talent, and that's a big fallacy that people make. I don't think soul has anything to do with talent. I've been on any number of buses where I've sat there and watched the bus driver greet people and I've said, "That's soul."

Lou Rawls plays in front of huge audiences. His soulfulness just has a bigger crowd. The woman driving the bus, her crowd's relatively small. That does not diminish the level of her soul or soulfulness. It does not diminish the risk on her part of putting herself out there, because there's no great applause. Any musician who moves ahead, who changes a bit, who doesn't play the greatest hits every time they're out there, they're taking risks. If you take a risk, no matter what it is in life – I don't even care if it is crossing against the red light when there's traffic coming – you're exhibiting part of your real self, whether it's the risk-taking aspect or you need to get across the street right now. It's energizing, it's emboldening, and it's real. You define soul, in many ways, as knowing (and this may be the hardest thing) what's real in yourself – and the willingness to display it in a genuine fashion.

Wanyoike Mbugua

SOULFUL MUSIC AROUND THE WORLD

The true beauty of music is that it connects people.

-Roy Ayers

DAVID BLOOM: Do you believe that there is a universality that is beyond language or culture? In other words, let's say jazz players went to China, and the people who listened to the concert hadn't heard jazz. Do you think it's possible for them to be moved or to have a soulful experience without the requisite background?

OSCAR BROWN, JR.: Every people around the world seem to have something that's music to their ears. Jazz seems to be music to many ears; it's not reciprocal. You listen to the music that comes from China or Japan, it's not going to move us the way our music might move them. That's why I'm attributing it to this rhythmic quality, because our bodies are polyrhythmic. You have a heartbeat, you have a pulse going on. You're breathing at a certain rhythm if you're walking. All of these rhythms are happening at once. Swing tends to address those in a way that evokes response, but I know a whole bunch of people here that still don't pat their feet. It just doesn't matter to them.

Look at the samba. Samba has had such an influence. We no longer even refer to it as samba. It's come into the culture to the point where it's just played, and we don't say here's a samba from Brazil. It's just there. One of the things about music is people will copy what they hear if they enjoy it. Then they'll try to duplicate it, replicate it or even create beyond that – put their own twist to it. That seems to be always happening.

Soul is like the blues. It's just a name that you attach to a certain style of music. You wouldn't say anything Shostakovich wrote was exactly soulful. You wouldn't say that a Bach Chorale was soulful. It's something different, and the styles of music change. Have you ever heard much classical music that swung?

DAVID BLOOM: Can forms of music that don't have an African influence be soulful?

OSCAR BROWN, JR.: I'm not referring strictly to black music or jazz music or even American music. I want soul. I showed you a lyric from "Clair de Lune," Jacques Brel. There's a universality of the spirit of the music that I want to create that overcomes ugliness with beauty, that overcomes a lie with the truth, that seeks a harmony to instruct the world, to serenade the world, to organize people.

TED COHEN: I like soul singers, and I like other kinds of singers. I like soul players, and I like other kinds of players. There's more soul, in a simple sense of this word, in a Puccini opera than there is a Mozart opera. You think Puccini's a better composer than Mozart, you're an idiot. There is feeling in the Mozart, but it comes through differently.

Let me give you kind of a complicated example. There's a very famous opera by Mozart called "Don Giovanni." It's Mozart's version of the Don Juan legend, and Don Juan, Don Giovanni, is out to seduce women. He's got this servant named Luparello. At a very famous point in the opera, what Don Giovanni wants is to get at this woman's maid. He's already seduced the woman. Now he wants the maid. He's got to get her out of the way, so he sends Luparello out to seduce this woman by singing to her. In this very famous scene, Luparello is standing there pretending to sing to her. The staging has to be good. The guy really singing and really playing the mandolin is Don Giovanni. He's hidden, and it all works.

What you're seeing here is that, given the music, even Luparello, who is kind of a clod, can seduce an aristocratic woman. The music is being given to him by Don Giovanni. You don't have to be the most astute observer of this opera to then have pop into your head: Where in the hell is Don Giovanni's music coming from? The answer is it's all coming from Mozart. Mozart's telling you something really deep about what he does. About what his life in music is. About what feelings he's expressing. Do you think that Mozart was a seducer? Do you think that Mozart had the feelings of a woman whose life has been ruined because her husband is a philanderer? No, of course not, but he knows what it sounds like. It makes him a genius.

OSCAR BROWN, JR.: Mozart and Beethoven and all these people who followed them came up with melodic stuff with really complex musical ideas. None of it swung. None of it ever had a pulse. Beethoven and the Ninth Symphony. He gets on a two-four thing that allows for a certain kind of physical movement, suggests it. When you look at European classical ballet, never is its movement rooted in rhythm. It moves to melody. It moves to mood. It moves to anything but a beat that is discernible. By the time you get to Gershwin, now you're off into something that is really swinging, has a beat, but has classical dimensions to it.

That development seems to have come into music following slavery with the infusion of Africans, particularly into America where they then began to draw on the music that was brought to America by all of the people who came from all the places in Europe with all their music. They came from Poland, they came from France, they came from England, they all brought their ditties from Spain, and everybody had their music. There was no such thing as an American music. The thing that tended to Americanize it was the African influence that it got in terms of tempo and rhythm, which was always resisted. Ragtime: They said the resentment almost drowned out the music.

John Coltrane

COLTRANE AND THE AVANT GARDE

OSCAR BROWN, JR.: Going back to the earlier time of music, at the point where music became soulful, an avant-garde attack was made on jazz by people who did not play soulfully, whose music was kind of hard to figure out where they were coming from. It seemed to have its genesis around Coltrane. Coltrane had a coherence that others didn't. All of a sudden, you start getting Cecil Taylor and Archie Shep and Sun Ra and people who are playing simultaneously but not together.

DAVID BLOOM: Coltrane gave license to many musicians to do just about anything without regard for the legacy of music. Yet to anyone who listens to him carefully, Coltrane was an incredible composer and improviser.

OSCAR BROWN, JR.: I worked with Coltrane at the Apollo. At the time, this was one of my first gigs.

DAVID BLOOM: Which year was that?

OSCAR BROWN, JR.: 1960, 1961. I was on with Coltrane and Miriam Makeba. It was a Symphony Sid production, eclectic like a big dog. I didn't understand Coltrane; he was playing all kinds of confused stuff to me. What in the hell is that? Max Roach and some of the other people I was talking to were telling me I was square. My ears had to sharpen up to check this out, so I tried. It was like classical music to a certain extent. I was only mildly successful.

I accosted Coltrane backstage. I said, "John, I think that as artists what we're supposed to be doing is communicating with the people. If we really have something to say, we should make it simple so they can understand it. It has profundity going for it. The people who seem to be complicating music and making it all that complex are really masking the fact that they don't have that much to say. What do you think?"

He says, "I'm kind of hoggish. I'm trying to find something on my horn, and I'm not that much concerned with the audience. When I was with Miles…" (He had his own group at this point) "…I knew that Miles and Cannonball were taking care of the entertainment part of it. I'm looking for something on my horn, and that's what my focus is." I said, "Cool. That means you ain't even talking to me. If I get it, it's just incidental to you, because you're just playing for yourself. I feel no obligation to understand something that's not even directed to me." That's how I felt.

Bit by bit, I began to dig Coltrane.

M Madpic

NEW GENERATIONS

OSCAR BROWN, JR.: Every new generation comes along with its own version of what music is. Usually it is resented by the earlier generation. It has to fight its way in. It gets established, and then something new comes along. What my parents were doing was the Charleston. They didn't understand jitterbug. What is that? When my kids came along, hip hop. What the hell is that? You call that music? Each generation seems to have its own peculiarities that it defends.

DAVID BLOOM: And nostalgia too.

OSCAR BROWN, JR.: Yeah, although I was telling my kids with hip hop, how you going to be nostalgic about that stuff? I had Duke Ellington. I had Woody Herman. What do you got?

DAVID BLOOM: I think it's very troubling. I look at the 1960s. I was a teenager then, and I feel personally for black music – in terms of rhythm and blues and jazz – I'd argue it was some of the best music of the last century. When I listen to today's music, I find that there's no romance, or very little.

OSCAR BROWN, JR.: All of a sudden, there are no melody lines. All of a sudden the beat went elsewhere and, to a certain extent, has stayed there. Even coherent musicians have become incoherent in the course of things. Herbie Hancock, I went to a concert down at Orchestra Hall. Four bars in, I knew I wasn't going to like this. They weren't saying anything that I understood. I couldn't even find a one. I knew that the drummer didn't have it. I looked at Herbie's foot; he wasn't patting on the one. If he was on the one, nobody else had a clue. They were just out there playing.

DAVID BLOOM: It's like the emperor's new notes.

OSCAR BROWN, JR.: Yeah, come on fellas! What are we doing? What am I supposed to get from this? I grew up with music impressing me. When I heard the blues, oh man, you could feel that. It'd give you something you could actually get into. Music and jazz could do that. You could be ever so miserable; the minute you walk in, the music starts jamming and your whole thing lifts. It just changes you. It has a spiritual quality that is hard to define.

DAVID BLOOM: You wouldn't say 'soulful' quality?

OSCAR BROWN, JR.: That's a name. You can call it whatever you want. The quality sometimes appears soulful – like what the jockey is wearing. Music comes in as a physical presence. Sounds, notes, impact on your canal receptors and send the information through the little hairs and fibers through your inner ear into the dendrites of your brain. That information is stored up in there. It collects in there, and if you are trained in a certain way, it evokes a certain bump, a certain feeling in you. The music rides in like a horse, but the spiritual quality rides in like a jockey. The physical part goes into the stable and the jockey goes into the clubhouse and has drinks.

DAVID BLOOM: Do you think a lot of musicians coming out now just don't have the background to play soulfully?

DON MEADE: Stylistically, no, because they've been influenced to go beyond swing and bebop – and have been taught this. They don't have the surety; it's all experimentation. But it can be less experimental if you take those elements with you as you march along that journey, along that road. Never forget where you came from. It's about where you're at in this time and place, and what you bring to that table.

DAVE LIEBMAN: The Western world is in a little funk now. This is true. But we had three, four hundred years. It's like jazz. We talk about jazz, how it's kind of an old thing. Listen man, the '60s, '70s and '80s, we were working every day, everywhere recording fourteen records a day. We had our fun. We had our party – party's over. I think we are in a transition period. A lot of it is because technology is way ahead of what we can deal with. It seems that the swing era was the last time that jazz was popular. After that, it's been underground, but when we were growing up it was a fairly good underground.

DAVID BLOOM: Exactly.

DAVE LIEBMAN: Underground is gone.

DAVID BLOOM: Everything is mainstream and everything is mainline now. It's the system. Everybody is getting the same information. It's hard to separate the trash from the positive. Our generation had to look for things because they weren't available. These guys now have everything on the phone and literally in their hands, and they have too much. You need to get rid of all that in order to know what you want to play – and what you want to say – to ultimately get back to soul. I think that's the problem of this generation: too many choices.

DAVE LIEBMAN: On the other hand, talking about jazz, for example, we are in the best state musically that's ever been. The young people are completely educated, and they are way better than I was at that age. They have all the opportunity in the world to learn and push a button and get the stuff that we used to write out. Those that want to do a career will take care of business. In a certain way, it's the most positive time for jazz I think I've ever seen. Like, "Where did you get that?" "I don't know. On YouTube when I was eleven. I saw John Coltrane and I copied it." I couldn't do that in my pajamas in my bedroom. This is a yin and yang all the time. It's always the positive and negative, dancing around.

DAVID BLOOM: Many musicians have virtuoso instrumental technique. But my problem is I don't hear… I don't hear much… I don't hear…

DAVE LIEBMAN: You don't hear much soul.

DAVID BLOOM: I don't hear soul.

Amelia Earhart

SOUL WITHOUT NOTES

The mother art is architecture. Without an architecture of our own we have no soul of our own civilization.

-Frank Lloyd Wright

DAVID BLOOM: Do you feel that art is inherently meaningless and false if it's not soulful?

STUDS TERKEL: I don't know what that means. There are two paintings on the wall here. There's one there by a friend of ours who died, Shelly Kent. Now that's a mother, an Indian-type mother, and a child against her breast. There's another one by Bruegel, a reproduction; the original would be millions, a Bruegel wedding. Where's the groom? You can't find the groom. The groom is there pouring whisky, pouring wine for the others. Well, they're both full of soul: one has a sweet tenderness to it, the other has a whimsical kind of lustiness to it, and both are soulful.

DAVID BLOOM: Would you say all art can communicate soul?

STUDS TERKEL: All art in one form or another – even the drippings of Jackson Pollock – could be soulful. To him certainly. And to those who dig it. I don't quite dig Pollack, but it's there.

ELSA MORA: When I was living in Cuba, in 1992, I was going through a very hard time. I had just graduated from the art school. The country was in a very difficult situation, a big crisis. People used to call that period "Option Zero." We didn't have any food. The transportation was horrible. I was living in a very small place. I was really desperate. I didn't have any money.

I didn't have anything. My brother had left the country in a very crazy way – in a boat – so I was really depressed. I even thought about committing suicide.

I thought I have to do something. I have to create something. I started working on a little painting. I remember very well that the title was "All You Have is Your Soul, Todo Lo Que Tienes Es Tu Alma." This was a very small figure, a woman without arms but with many feathers. I was just trying to forget about everything and focus on this little painting, and I realized that during the process, I was getting stronger and stronger. I thought wow, this is very funny. My soul just saved my life, because I was realizing that in the end, when you're lost, desperate, depressed, you still have that little something called soul. It's something that you can never lose. You can lose all the material things in your life, your hopes, everything, but you don't ever lose that thing that is really the essence of what you are.

BILL KURTIS: The first time I walked into the Sistine Chapel, I had no idea about art. I had no training. I had vaguely heard about the Sistine Chapel; I had no idea what it was. And I opened the door, about the size of a regular door, and looked up and here were Michelangelo's frescoes stretching down the ceiling and then "The Last Judgment" at the other end. It so moved me that I went back and researched every Michelangelo piece in existence, and wrote a book about it – which I never published. But how's that for making an impact?

Beauty of whatever kind, in its supreme development, invariably excites the sensitive soul to tears.

-Edgar Allan Poe

TED COHEN: Emotion that just bursts out usually doesn't give you a lot of art. It has to be controlled, shaped in some way in order to have any real endurance. For example, was Mark Twain soulful? I think so, but there's so much art in what he does that sometimes it's kind of hard to tell. When he lets down his guard and the art goes away, then he's not too good. He just starts yelling, railing against God. He hated Mary Baker Eddy. You know, he wrote a whole book attacking the Christian Science Church. That's not good at all. He was just enraged. But he's got it in *Huckleberry Finn*. There's no question. Yeah, I think he was soulful.

DAVID BLOOM: As a writer, what inspired you?

OSCAR BROWN, JR.: I started writing songs as a teenager. Actually, I wrote a poem when I was about twelve years old that my parents made part of their Christmas card. I continued to write from time to time as I grew up. Pretty soon it became a hobby, a serious hobby. A girl would break my heart, I'd write a heartbroken song. Then I would sing it with my friends at gatherings. I didn't have that much of a voice at that point, but I was a composer. I was original, so they tolerated me.

I'm writing this song now called "Why Do We Call Them the Blues?" Why is that color the one we choose when we say we feel low? Why do we call them the blues when we're describing our miserable moods? Would people know what we meant if we said we felt low down and green? It could be red. It could be purple. It's just nomenclature.

BILL KURTIS: I wrote a book on the death penalty because of soul. I knew it wouldn't be a best seller. I mean, you're not going to curl up with the death penalty before you go to bed at night. But I did it because I felt right about doing it, I felt I should do it, I felt moved. I said, "This is going to be ultimately a success because I did it for the right reason." And so the gauge, if you will, that I apply to what I do, what stories I cover, is whether it touches something inside me. But I have to have that feeling before I really commit fully to it. Otherwise, I'm just making money.

ANDREA COSNOWSKY: After college I became a songwriter. I was writing songs because I loved to write. There's was nothing else in the world I'd rather be doing, I didn't even realize where the time had gone, because I had been in another place. To me that was bliss, because I was not conscious of my surroundings, I was so focused in the moment.

When I got my first songwriting job, I had quotas, and I always had this nagging thought in the back of my mind: What would so and so think about this chorus? What are they going to think about this verse? I wonder who I can write this song for. I never was able to get to that place where I was so happy, because I was now doing this as a business. I was more about trying to please the outside, and I had lost what really made me happy about songwriting.

DAVID BLOOM: I know soul is connected to music and art, but what about other endeavors? Can soul be found in the judicial system?

BLANCHE MANNING: There have been times as a judge when I've had cases where I had difficulty containing my emotions. When I was practicing law as a prosecutor, I had a murder case. The young man who was charged was unable to explain his whereabouts on the evening in question. My supervisor suggested that I should ask for the death penalty, but I felt I couldn't do that because we had a purely circumstantial case. We had no direct evidence of the young man's involvement, although he was there. His blood was on the victim. Her blood was on him. His shoe was next to her body. He was in the vicinity.

In interviewing witnesses, I had an inner sense that something was awry, something was wrong. I went ahead and tried the case because we had some evidence. But we didn't have sufficient evidence to ask for a death penalty. The jury came back with the verdict in ten minutes, and they wanted to know why we didn't ask for the death penalty. I was really concerned about this young man, and I was concerned about the victim too. She had been heinously and brutally murdered, but I didn't think he did it. Consequently, I told the judge that I was not going to participate in the sentencing process. I was that emotional about it.

A year later I got a call from the judge asking me had I read the paper. It turned out that somebody else confessed to the murder. My defendant had received two hundred years in jail but, obviously, he was released with some kind of compensation. I was very emotional about the case. It was what you might call a soul situation.

There have been many times over the years that I've had to impose long prison sentences on young people. That hurts my heart. I think it's important that people in a courtroom situation realize that the judge considers them to be real people, human beings who have feelings. Sometimes I just sit there and think: But for the grace of God, there goes my kid. It's really very difficult. Sometimes their families are out in the courtroom, and you see them weeping and it really tugs at your heart. Obviously, if they have committed a crime, there's got to be punishment. The court is compelled to abide by the law and impose that punishment, but it doesn't feel good. It's very emotional.

I consider myself to be an extremely soulful person both in terms of what happens here in the courtroom as a judge and also what happens when I am playing a musical instrument.

BILL KURTIS: We do a lot of crime shows now. And the best interviews are always the people who are eyewitnesses to an accident, or reflecting on their own experience. So they're not worrying about how they are perceived or look to someone else, but just give it to you straight. There is a truthfulness that is hard to get away from. Soulfulness is people connecting with people. And it can be a rare insight that can be communicated in a phrase or a pause.

Each of us within our individual vocation can find soul. I have it here in creating documentaries. I have a composer, an audio director who makes the music. I write the words, I record the words, he performs the music. And then we have cameramen who are capturing the pictures. Editors who put them together. And once in a while, we touch that thing called soul in our craft, our art, and when it happens I call everybody into this room and I say, "This is it." It all comes together as one universal moment. The picture is there, that's good. The music absolutely fits the picture. The written words evoke not information, but a feeling.

STUDS TERKEL: I'm celebrated for having celebrated the non-celebrated. So that's the exquisite irony. Well, of course, what I'm trying to say is that in everyone there is some kind of possibility, whether it comes through or not. A lot depends on circumstances. See this one guy, this laborer says, "Sometime I'll be forgotten, but I'd like to see a piece of metal on the top of a skyscraper. The bottom has an architect's name, Frank Lloyd Wright, Mies van der Rohe, but I'd like to see a piece of metal from the fiftieth floor to the bottom with the name of every guy who hung iron, every carpenter, scrubwoman, every stenographer, every elevator operator, so I could say I did that, I was there." That's what it's about.

BILL HORBERG: I've always tried to have a very outward posture towards the whole world and wanted to look beyond the borders of my experience of my neighborhood, my city, my family, my religion, and really get out into a deeper explanation of the Earth that we're on – and the people that are on it, the multifarious and multicolored shades of human experience.

Another world can be a world of the past, could be a world of the future. It could be a world outside of our borders. It could be a microcosm within our own society. But I'm fascinated by those borders and by the transgression of those borders, by stories of immigration and change and diaspora, by stories about changing identity. I guess that has also driven my film career and those projects that I naturally gravitate to. Soulfulness can be closely associated with artists who feel most strongly that communication of what is essential and what is true and what is deeply human and authentic through all the myriad ways of artistic expression: It can be filmmaking. It can be music. It can be painting. It can be storytelling. It can be something more performance-based – dance, obviously.

Dance is the hidden language of the soul of the body.

-Martha Graham

WENDY CLINARD: My history with dance began when it knocked on my door, so to speak. I was a ferocious painter. It was the thing that made sense to the adolescent: draw, draw, draw. Then I went to the Art Institute and paint, paint, paint. I really liked the human form. I've always liked working from life. Human beings were great to observe and work with two-dimensionally. Then I was in New York and a friend of mine was touring with a flamenco company, so I went to sketch the class. My sketches looked amazingly corny, but what I was seeing didn't feel corny to me. There was an immediate connection. It was visceral; even observing it was physical, very physical inside of me. I said, "Well, I think I'll just try to dance. I think I'll dance and maybe if I move, then I can figure out how to capture that as a painter." It was never a conscious thing until probably a dozen years later when I said to myself, "I guess I'm a dancer." But I still feel like my sensibility is more like a painter. I'm a painter who dances, I guess.

I'm really small. Being physical has always felt right. Then I started to open myself to the whole history of dance. That's when it becomes like, whoa! Someone actually said that with their body. You're like, if she did it, I'll try to do it and look for that thing too. The longer you stay in it, the stakes are just higher.

There are various "palos" in Flamenco. We call them "palo" rhythms. In a very simplified way, each "palo" embodies a certain human condition, like there's loneliness – and something like madness. There's, of course, "fiesta" and more playful forms. "Alegría" means happiness. There is a lot of that strong kind of thing. The physical way we're using it is from here, it's internal.

What does it feel like when I'm dancing? It depends on the performance. The times that you remember are the times when you barely remember anything. Those are the best ever. It's a really great thing to share with other people because everybody can identify. Everyone carries a body with them so there is something already shared from the very start.

NATALIJA NOGULICH: When you hear someone's voice that's really soulful, they're an unobstructed resonating chamber. They're just wide open, humming. And that's for any kind of performance, even an athletic performance – they're not in their own way. They're in what they call now – the popular term is "being in the zone." That just means you're not inhibited, you're not hampered. The trash has been swept away. And then, yeah, you are in a zone because you're clear. Soul is clarity, and it can be calm or it can be fierce. But it is true. That's the one word that would, for me, have to be included in my understanding of soul.

I was in my twenties, studying with David Mamet at the St. Nicholas Theater Company, when I realized that acting was living truthfully under the circumstances given to you in your play. It wasn't about pretending or believing or creating a feeling, and it's like I had a "ah ha" moment. I had a eureka moment where I thought, "Oh, my gosh! Now I get it. This what I'm meant to do. All I have to do is work hard for the rest of my life." And that was such a relief. It wasn't like a sense of, oh, man this is going to be like uphill; it was just the opposite. It was a leveling feeling of, oh, it's telling the truth. Then I realized I was home. I had a sense of home in the theater.

Every role I work on, I've got to find that connection to the train, you know, the truth train. I've got to hook on. Every role, or else you can't do it; you're just going to be BS'ing up there. Some years ago I was cast in the title role of Hedda Gabler. Which is a role like Hamlet is for men, Hedda is for women. And why? Well, you know, it's a four-act play. You're on stage the entire time. It's a journey from A to Z and back again. You have no idea at the beginning where things are going to end up for her – unless, of course, you know the play. But it's also a role that's done over and over again because it does have that depth.

What resonated for me about it, and I think I made some discoveries that I have not seen in other interpretations of Hedda, was that this character would rather not be than not be herself. And that was huge for me. I thought, "Yes! This is who I should be playing. And need to be playing. And need to find in whoever I play." And that wasn't just an expression or a thought. She lived it, she walked it. She takes her own life at the end of the play. The falsity of her marital status and the status in her life in 1889 in Norway, where a woman could not be her own person fully and have a place in society, was so false for her that she chose to not be.

She was the daughter of a general. She grew up around guns and horses and boots and men that her father would bring home to have cognac and cigars and smoke and listen. And she was smart. Where were they going to put a woman like this at that time? So she married. She married an academician who bored her to tears, and there was no way she could – she tried to do the expected. But finally, the expectation of herself, her authentic self, was what won. That voice won and it cost her her life. A very high price. Those kinds of challenges, the tuition is high, you know, as in very expensive school.

But, you know, she burned. She burned with fire through that play, searching to create a place, a space where she could be herself. I've seen that role done where she's played cold and distant. No. She didn't die of too much ice – she died of too much heat. Those are the roles, those are the yummy things that we get to do. You don't ever release a role completely, it just finds another place inside you to live because we're all humming with infinite possibilities.

I feel I'm very much myself on stage. I feel I live on stage. I feel at home on stage. I've always felt that. I feel soulfulness in my life – it's with me. Yes, I meditate, I pray. But it doesn't even have to be formed in that way. It's when I'm being truthful about what I want, what I'm going after. What I want to give, who I am. And I'm not trying to douse it or accommodate something outside. But when I'm really working from the inside out, whether it's a phone conversation or a role or teaching, is when I'm expressing soul. It's infinite. And it really is, in a certain way, the only reality. The rest of it's not real. So soul is not just for me on stage. But there's something about doing the words of a great writer that goes beyond what you experience in your ordinary life. There is something extraordinary about being on stage. Supra-ordinary.

PATTI VASQUEZ: Soulfulness is such a personal explanation; everyone has a different idea. It has a lot to do with what the universe says through you. We all have something to say, whether or not we find it. Soul is a big component of comedy. Comedy is a developmental thing and it takes a long time to find a voice that connects with humor, with what people have to say. When you start out it's hard to see the soul coming through – because you're trying to be funny. As you go on and find your voice and find the soul of comedy, it all comes together. It's a really beautiful thing to watch.

When you see someone like George Carlin or Richard Pryor or Bill Cosby or Ellen DeGeneres, it's obviously such a component of who they are. I love Jackie Mason. He's absolutely wonderful and such a nice man. George Carlin has such a connection with what he really believes and what he says. He's so quick at it, and he has such a huge amount of material. I don't think anybody has been as prolific as George Carlin. He really found himself.

People get uncomfortable in a comedy club. When they come to see a Patti Vasquez show, they surely know what to expect, and that's my experiences, as humiliating, embarrassing, and tough as they were. My frustrations are my humiliations. It is my persona which is like, I guess you would call me sassy. At one time I was just a gimmick. I'm Irish and Mexican and I could do my mom's accent. When I do a show, I can tell them that my father passed away and how it's changed my life, and still make it funny. Obviously, my father passing away isn't funny, but my dad had such a great sense of humor up until his last day.

"Pregnant Party Girl" came from what someone else called me when they saw me pregnant. I used to drink a lot and then I couldn't drink anymore. I'm not really a party girl. That doesn't fit me either. I guess my image continues to change, but the material keeps still. I keep building on that. You're trying to make things funny, which can sometimes take you away from the soul of what you're doing. The audience sometimes knows better than you do. Not all the time – but once in a while you just say something, not even intentionally, whether it's natural or you just stumble across it, and the audience really connects with it. That's an amazing thing. It really is.

What's funny to different people has to do with soul. It does have to do with your upbringing. Some people don't want to hear dirty words. Some people don't think that slapstick is funny, whether that's from your religious background or from just what you grew up around. Maybe talking about sex isn't comfortable for people. For me very little is out of bounds. I don't know why that is. Maybe it's from my upbringing. I've always been very honest. That's the only way I knew how to do comedy.

I love my audiences. Even if I'm not having a good time I never criticize them. I'm laying myself bare a lot because my stories, all my comedy, comes from personal experiences. It makes me very vulnerable. If they're not having a good time, I don't blame myself. That's not my fault or their fault. It just didn't happen. They're there to have a good time – and I'm doing my best. Sometimes you hit a line better than you've ever done it before. Sometimes you'll chase after that and try to do things exactly the same way again. But generally I've been enjoying the moment where I know it's better than it's ever been. I can't explain it. I can't describe it. It's like riding a wave through its crest. You can just sit there for a second while everyone's enjoying it.

ANDREA COSNOWSKY: Who wants to be a rabbi? That's such a nerdy thing. I originally felt twinges of the calling when I was in high school. I was around fifteen, sixteen but thought it was a lame position. I ran off and became a songwriter after college, and I was in Nashville, Tennessee, for nine years. Probably around the seventh year, the eighth year, I had this feeling that I wanted to do something bigger. It felt like I was mostly just living for myself and writing songs for me, even though I wanted to write songs to change the world. I didn't want it to be all about me anymore, so I said I wonder what else I could do. Never ask that question if you really don't want the answer, because when the answer came to become a rabbi, I thought what else could I do? I thought nope, there's nothing else I can do. This is where I'm supposed to be.

I've noticed that since I've left professional songwriting and gone into the rabbinate, my music has gotten back to that place of I do it because I love it. I've been more successful. What defines success? If you'd asked me that ten years ago, I would have said success is a big room full of people really appreciating what I do. Today it's more about what can I bring to my congregation with my music – and not about how they're going to take it. It's more of I am the vessel, and I will let God work through me to bring people closer to God. It's really not about me anymore. It's really about I'm here to be of service. I'm here as the vessel of God.

TOM BURRELL: If there is something in business that has surprised me, vis-à-vis this whole area of soul, it's probably more in the area of people and the effect that a person who is in business, particularly a person who is running a business, can have in people's lives in a qualitative way – beyond just providing salary and benefits. And I guess the thing that surprised me too is that, in the process of running a business, you are basically directing people and instructing and counseling people, and sometimes it can be pretty harsh. Sometimes you have to fire people, and sometimes you have to come down hard on people. One of the things that I have seen is that if you do it with a kind of purity of thought, a kind of soulfulness, if you will, it's picked up. People get it, people understand it.

I have had situations where I have had to let people go and, in the process, they have wound up having to console me, because they feel the pain that I am going through having to do that. Many people have come back and thanked me for what I said to them and for what I had to do, because that was kind of a wakeup call. There was something that needed to be fixed – and I went out and fixed it.

When a person has a job and you know that if you terminate that person they will never work in that business again, that says something about whether they should be working in the business, as opposed to saying, well, I have got to save this person from this fate. If the only reason they can be in the business is because you hired them, that may suggest that they should be looking for something else – and that should not be deferred or delayed. So the sooner you release that person, the sooner they can start searching for the truth about who they are – and pursue it.

TED COHEN: Philosophy is supposed to begin from nothing, right? It takes nothing for granted, makes no presuppositions and no assumptions. It starts at ground level, so that appealed to me. It looked like it would be a place in which I would be on all fours with everyone else.

I come from what by any reasonable standard is an academically and culturally deprived background. I have no regrets about my childhood at all, but the fact of the matter is that when I showed up at college I hadn't read the same books as other people. I didn't know what paintings were, although I had played some classical music in my high school band. I mispronounced the names of artists. I just didn't know stuff. Even other parts of my education were at best minimal: science and mathematics.

I spent a lot of time feeling inadequate around some really high-class kids who knew lots of stuff. I remember having a course in which we were going to study a Beethoven string quartet. When it was announced that that's what we were going to be studying next, there was a girl from Manhattan who said, "Oh, good old Opus 131." I thought Jesus, am I ever going to catch up? She knows the Opus? Now I know the Opus.

But I have a sort of natural instinct for argument, and that's what my kind of philosophy really is. I'm good at the technical parts of philosophy, the parts that involve mathematics and stuff. It's a good thing that I have an academic life. It suits me. It suits me because there's somebody who will employ me.

I had a student once whose father told him that none of the really great philosophers were in universities. "Kid," I said, "that's almost but not quite true. It's true up until the middle part of the 18th century, and then Comte, Hegel, and all those people start being in universities. What your father's not paying attention to is that universities are now the patrons. There didn't used to be composers in universities. There didn't used to be painters or poets, but there are now. We don't have nobleman. We don't have somebody like the earl of wherever the hell it was that would take the great philosopher, David Hume, and support him, so I had to go to a university. Fortunately, it's here. This place and I suit one another very well. There are a million things wrong with the University of Chicago, but they don't bother me too much. What's good about the place is just what I need.

ERWIN DRECHSLER: I always loved food and I always loved wine, and I loved education. Having the restaurant and being involved in food and wine and working with people is an extension of my background, because I'm always trying to better what I can do and what our staff can do in terms of knowledge, in terms of nurturing our customers.

I think my feeling of soulfulness about food really started when I was a kid growing up at home. My parents were from Eastern Europe; my mom was from Austria, my father was from Czechoslovakia. They came here after World War II. My memories of eating at home were always of things that were homemade, made from scratch. My mom was an incredible baker. So there was always some bread on the table. There was also some baked food for dessert. When we sat at the dinner table, there was no TV, there was no radio, and everything stopped. It was a time to be with family. It was a time to appreciate the food on the table. I don't think I was aware of it, it was just unconscious, but this was how food should be. It should be simple. It should be fresh. It should be flavorful. It should be what it originally started out to be – and not manipulated at all.

I think that people who grow up with food as an integral part of their community and family have a different sense of appreciation for what that product is. There is a movement and awareness in people that it is important to eat food in a healthy way, in an unprocessed way. That transcends into what we do here. We have a philosophy that less is more. The less that you manipulate food, the more you are able to enjoy what that food is about.

Nurturing seems to be, for me, a key word. It's not just nurturing in terms of food; it's nurturing one's soul. It's not necessarily about people coming in here and saying, "I'm hungry. I want to eat something," it's coming in here and being taken care of. It's creating an atmosphere where people can feel comfortable, where they can talk with one another, where they can share their experiences during that day. Our focus is about flavors. It's about layers. It's about composition. That's really my passion here, our passion.

SOUL TO SOUL

Juan Pablo Rodriguez

Soul can be selfish when it isn't shared. Once a person realizes that others experience similar feelings, compassion is born. People interviewed for this chapter ask numerous questions and provide provocative answers: Does soul exist without empathy? Can a prejudiced person still be soulful? Revealing one's soul demands risk-taking and the willingness to be vulnerable. "There but for the grace of God…" begets charity and personal growth.

In this chapter we discover how soul listens as much as it speaks. Successful performers connect directly with their audiences, psychotherapists with their patients, teachers with their students. Many people have experienced an occasion when, on meeting someone new, they instantly recognized a familiar soul, possibly a person they knew in a previous life.

Person-to-person connections engender good deeds – and sometimes acts of evil. In the realms of education and politics, souls may be touched, but they may also be destroyed. In the American judicial system, rigid sentencing guidelines test the limits of soul. Battling the ease of first impressions, soulful people dig deeper and – seeing themselves in others – come to see their own souls.

RICK KOGAN: We all wind up at the same place, and the richness of life and the joy of life is what kind of journey you make it. And you are the person who gets to make it. Nobody gets to make it for you. Other people can influence it. You can have wonderful companions along for the ride.

Let my soul smile through my heart and my heart smile through my eyes, that I may scatter rich smiles in sad hearts.
-Paramahansa Yogananda

RICK KOGAN: I was arrested in Florida in 1969 for a modest drug thing. Given my life before that, I was a relatively privileged young man. And we were, for a variety of circumstances, thrown in jail, Dade County Jail. Walking up into the cell before we were bailed out (it was a Sunday – and relatively difficult to do), I was as terrified as I've ever been before or since. As I was walking up there, I was talking to this bulky black guard and I started crying. I said, "Please don't do this! Please don't put me in there, I beg you!" And every time before, that kind of thing had worked for me. "I can't be in here!" I was so scared. Terrified! And this guard, I wish I knew his name, he took me aside. Another guard, it was a white guard, said, "Get him in there!" The first guard said, "I want to talk to this young man." He took me aside, he took me around the corner. This was a no-bullshit kind of place. And he said, "Look, young man, I don't want to do this to you. You seem like a nice young man, and you're going in a cell with thirty people, who are not nice people. You have got to stop crying, you have got to dry your tears. And you have got to be strong. I went through the same thing you're going through right now when I was a young man, and I have been fine ever since."

And he gave me the sleeve of his uniform. (I was 17 years old and the captain of the football team at my high school.) He dried my tears, while this other jerk is screaming, "Come on, come on! Get him in here!" He dried my tears on the sleeve of his shirt and said, "Let's just wait, let's just wait. When you go in there, you tell them it was cocaine, if they ask what you got arrested for. Don't swear at these guys. Don't be adversarial. Don't you try to be a football player. You just go in there. And you must know: Maybe it's tomorrow, maybe it's going to be another day from now, but your parents, they're going to bail you out. And [when they do], I want you to just look at the sun, look at something that makes you happy, because this world, it's going to be a happy place for you." I have never, ever, forgotten that. It got me through one of the worst times in my life.

Was that man soulful? I think he was sharing a part of himself that he didn't need to. [He could've just] thrown me in jail, that's what they do: throw people in jail. He did not need to do that. He took it upon himself, for nothing. There's nothing in this for him. I have never heard of him, or saw him after that day.

CHARLES JAFFE: Empathy is all about using your own personal emotional range and your own personal experience to compare and contrast with another person's. You do that in a dialog, and you come to know another person's inner self more and more accurately. You can't do that without really giving yourself over to the experience. There are certain things that have come up again for me very powerfully in that way. Essential things about myself: fears, ideals, pieces of my own personal history that I know have changed me that have gone well beyond words.

JEWEL TANCY: Whatever goes on in my life, I try to think about other people in their lives and the fact that they're probably going through the same thing that I'm going through. So I just write a letter, I write a song about it. "This Moment" is a piece I wrote at a time when someone came into my life and was there for me in a way that I never thought could happen. Oh, I get emotional when I think about that: having someone just appear in your life. As many people say, a stranger is a friend you never met.

Friendship is a single soul dwelling in two bodies.

-Aristotle

TED COHEN: I've had friends who seemed to me deeply compassionate and caring people who understood things about how other people felt sooner than most people do. The kind of person who, when he does something that affects you, is able to vividly imagine how this is going to feel to you. It's a human job to understand the rest of the world. It's harder than it sounds to accept the fact that other people are different than you and not therefore worse.

ELSA MORA: I don't like to just close doors and say no. You know, gay people, no. People with surgeries, no. No, the opposite. Those are people too, and they're exactly me. The same material, so I'm just curious. I want to explore into those people's soul, because it is different. That is why I'm very open to difference with any kind of person. I don't have any problem with that. I'm super curious. I like people. I love people, and I think the more open I am to them, the better person I am, because I understand more.

RICK KOGAN: Can people be soulful without any connection to another person? I think not. The ways in which we communicate on any level are what define this indefinable word called soul. Most people believe it's kind of a spiritual or quasi-spiritual thing that's inside everybody. It is everybody. It is the whole package. How you choose to display that package is totally up to you. It is, I suppose, in the way you dress, in the way you speak, in what you do. But it's all this need to communicate with other people, to share. Every person is unique. If you are willing to share some part of you, if you feel – in the most genuine way – that something you're sharing is real, freighted with all the bullshit that comes along with life, then you are soulful. Whether someone responds to you or not is really kind of immaterial.

That level of communication you cannot buy and you cannot fake. I'm one of the great bullshitters of all time. You know, it's my business, as a reporter, to know somebody quick, get what I want, and get out. When it's for real, when you make that connection, it cannot be genuine without a sharing of what people believe is their real self. That, indeed, may be what soul is all about: communicating – on that strange, buried, complicated, screwed-up level – what you believe.

ANDREA COSNOWSKY: When you talk about having a soul communication with someone, I feel that souls are familiar with each other. For instance, if you've ever met someone that you've never met before, but you have an instant connection to them, it's that your soul recognizes their soul. We might have never met before, but our souls once knew each other on some level in the past. Sometimes I've had experiences where I can look into my dog's eyes and feel like I know what the dog was thinking – but not so much with people.

RICK KOGAN: There's an element of vulnerability when anybody shares a piece of themselves that is genuine; they automatically are making themselves vulnerable. If a bus driver says nothing, the person looks right through the bus driver and moves on. If the bus driver says, "Hi, how are you this morning?" it begs a person, it opens up to "What do you care? Why don't you shut up?!" It makes life a little more dangerous, to exhibit soul. I don't think anybody has ever been soulful without huge risk involved.

Ordinary riches can be stolen, real riches cannot. In your soul are infinitely precious things that cannot be taken from you.

-Oscar Wilde

BOB WILLEMS: Your soul on its own doesn't do much. I think it's interactive, the purpose of humanity. Apart from any specific religion or any specific spiritual voice, you got to believe on some level there's a reason that there's five billion people on the planet – and we're all trying to find some way to get along.

Is each individual supposed to be off on their own little thing and try to pursue like, "I'm a musician. I'm going to practice many hours a day but I'm never going to share it with anybody." No. The whole purpose of most of the very important things that people are going to achieve in their lives involves interacting with others.

If I'm on a mission to find what's in my heart, what's my soul all about, and what are the absolutely fundamental important things to me – if I get some answers to these questions, I want to share them. When you discover these things, you want to share them with others in a compassionate way and a way that's not hesitant or under heavy consideration. You're just openly sharing yourself with somebody else what's important to you and what values are important to you. That can change people's lives, and it can change them in a very profound way.

CHRISSY DELACOTTA: As I tend to meet new and interesting people and broaden my horizons, I find more and more of myself in other people. When you meet more people and you get more experience, you tend to look back at yourself and reflect: Okay, what does this have to do with me? How have I grown, or what have I learned from these people? I think as you do that, you find yourself – and you find your soul.

RICK KOGAN: If I meet someone new, or I walk in a lobby, if I'm feeling lousy, I look at the guard and go, "This guy's got a lousier job than I do." Why would I walk by this guy without saying "Hi?" And I see it happen all the time. Okay, that's not the highest level of communication, saying hi to a guard. But, you know, three months later, you'll have a conversation with him and learn something. It's a great thing! I think it is the ability to share a genuine part of who you really are, and to share it in a way that begs people to share back. It is an entreaty. It is an offering: "Here I am."

ANN SAWYER: There are homeless people or people who are not very well off in the world, and there are people who take the time to pull out some money and give them some. Sometimes if you just see someone even cast a smile at someone, I think that is showing kindness and soulfulness.

Gratitude is the fairest blossom which springs from the soul.

-Henry Ward Beecher

RICK KOGAN: Soul has a lot to do with the world around you. If you are unwilling to connect – I don't even care if it's some slight sociopath like Miles Davis, who will turn his back on the audience – you don't want to connect? Don't play on a stage! Go play in your closet! You are putting yourself out there, you are allowing yourself to be vulnerable in front of other people, in what I think is an inherently human and desperate need to connect with the world around you, even if it's one person. The more, obviously, the merrier.

DAVE LIEBMAN: You take into account the audience. You look out and get a feel for the place, its ambience. We are playing for more and more gray-haired people, and that means jazz is having difficulty reaching young people – for a variety of obvious reasons. We're playing for people what they've heard as teenagers, and that stays with them for the rest of their lives. It evokes memory, nostalgia and just a good vibe. Whether it's Coltrane, or The Beatles or some folk singer or Tchaikovsky, it's the same thing.

On the other hand, I try to push the audience a little further to understand what we do: hopefully to higher levels of feelings, and deeper levels of feelings. If you can sit up there and sing and have thirty people sobbing at what you did, you have connected with them and you have made them vulnerable, too – and you have touched their souls. As much as I think we're artists and creative, we are still entertainers, and as soon as somebody pays one penny to see you, you're there to make them feel good.

PATTI VASQUEZ: We want to touch each other's souls but we don't think it on a conscious level. For me as a comic, I hope that people see themselves by sharing myself. Maybe they'll feel better about certain things. I tell a lot of humiliating experiences. I have material about women's exams. Some people told me that when they're in the stirrups they think of me and laugh, which may not be something that you really want to hear. I laugh a lot on stage, too. I giggle at myself, at embarrassing things. I like to laugh with the audience. Sometimes when they laugh, they make me laugh. It's so wonderful.

DAVID BLOOM: What does it tell you about the world when they're laughing?

PATTI VASQUEZ: You can't think of anything else when you're laughing at something. For the moment everything's okay. I've had people who told me that they've had tough times in their life recently and it's their first time getting out. They are really glad to have a laugh.

DAVID BLOOM: One thing that I learned about my dad, who died of Alzheimer's a few years ago: For his last eight years, we didn't have any real verbal conversations. There were responses and smiles, but when he was getting to the end of the road, I had an epiphany. We were in a restaurant and he was just looking blank. All of a sudden he started laughing, this deep laugh. I realized at that point that there is no better statement of well-being than a hearty laugh. When that laugh happens, at that moment, everything is okay.

PATTI VASQUEZ: The world is good.

DAVID BLOOM: When the world isn't so good and people need therapy, how does that affect a psychiatrist's soul?

CHARLES JAFFE: What washes over me all the time is a feeling of humility at bearing witness to people coming to know and exposing their fundamental core experiences of themselves and the world, and their relationships with other people. The whole package, the process of people exposing themselves, the willingness to make themselves open in the presence of another person, the profound humility and privilege of bearing witness to that kind of thing. That is the highest level of people immersing themselves with each other, and to me that's very soulful, very essentially expressive.

RICK KOGAN: You think people miss the essence a lot? I think people miss the essence almost all the time. They're judging on the first impression: What does this person do? What does this person say? Somewhere along the line we've gotten out of the business of accepting people on face value, taking the person for not what they seem to be, but who they are. A person is not what they wear, a person is not what they do.

Most encounters are the most superficial kinds of encounters you'll find anywhere. "Hi, what do you do? What are you doing?" It's the same kind of thing you find in every office. Monday, people will say to you, "How was your weekend?" They don't really care. Most of the time, if you said, "Well, my mom died and I went out and robbed a bank," they'll say, "Yeah, mine was okay too." It's a superficial way of living that I think is getting increasingly so. Somewhere along the line we forgot how to talk to each other as human beings. We're afraid of each other. We're afraid to show someone who we are. So why would we expect someone to show us who they are, if we're not reciprocating in kind or making an offering of sorts?

The easiest thing in the world is to ask someone a question. The worst they can do is say no; then that's it! All you're saying about yourself is you're interested enough in that other person to want to know something.

JEWEL TANCY: When one person's soul touches another, you're saying basically everybody's got soul, but there's a certain amount that people let out. You meet someone on the street. You bump into that person. "Oh, excuse me." You see someone you haven't seen in five years. "Hey, how are you doing?" "I'm doing okay." They're kind of holding back. They're not going to tell you, "Hey, I just got out of jail. I just robbed a bank." No, they say, "I just… You know, life is good. I've got the kids in the house with a picket fence and a dog named Fido."

When you have a conversation with someone, you should be listening to what they're saying. Try to understand what they're saying. You should be talking with them, not always to them – something we all need to work on. It depends on the amount of what's being shared, what's being given, what's being received. It's funny. I don't think you can really expect too much all the time. As far as people go, we need to just go moment by moment. That's really embracing soul.

RICK KOGAN: Genuine soul, revealed, makes the world a better place. It makes everyone you encounter, whether it's in a jazz club, or an art gallery, or on a piece of paper, feel better about themselves, feel connected somehow to this secret soul world that exists all over this planet.

DAVID BLOOM: What sorts of things do people say when they're revealing the secrets of their souls? Do people tell you anything when they're silent?

CHARLES JAFFE: Absolutely. The true currency in this room [a psychiatrist's office] is emotion, and words are ways to capture it as best as words can. Some of the most profound experiences begin where words end. People change in this room oftentimes during moments of silence where there's a washing over both of us of the real depth of meaning of what's going on. Yeah, words are vectors. Words are indexes. They're signs. They're symbols to capture that emotion.

When we learn to speak and we go to school and we learn how to get along with Johnny and Mary, we learn that we're not supposed to be completely spontaneous about our innermost selves. That doesn't work for social ritual. We learn to use words to not reveal ourselves, and part of what the search for one's innermost being is about is really using words in a different kind of service, which people are very, very loathe to do. It's hard, because it's full of embarrassment and shame and self-consciousness. That's why, I guess, many people find using nonverbal means a little easier, because it's not quite so laden with all those inhibitions.

There can be a deep sharing of an essence without words at all. And a deep sense of inner understanding that has nothing to do with words.

BILL HORBERG: A lot of my journey through life has been one of getting to understand myself in a deeper and more complex way, of going within to find myself through the accumulated experiences of my life – something in the DNA, some essential truth to who I am. I'm trying to get comfortable with that and find ways to communicate that and connect with other people in a very honest and authentic way, whether that's verbal communication, or nonverbal communication – whether it's musical – the sublimity of a moment or of a vision of artistic beauty. I think of it in terms of a desire that we all have to connect on some deep level with other people and to find a way to communicate what is within ourselves – to express what can be termed soul.

DAVID BLOOM: Can soul be expressed through actions, like good deeds?

CLIFF COLNOT: I don't feel discussing soulful acts is soulful, so I won't answer that. The notion that I would answer by saying, "Why yes, in 1972, I remember that I went down to the West Side and helped somebody move out of their crib and bought them new furniture to move into their new place. I thought that was quite soulful. And then I remember in 1984, I gave an entire Thanksgiving dinner to a single parent in the Cabrini Green projects, and I felt particularly good about that. I mean, I felt wow, Cliff, you're really soulful." The idea of reciting instances of soulfulness would instantly contaminate your credibility as being soulful.

TED COHEN: We always pay attention to people's motives. Sometimes we figure out right. It makes a difference why people do what they do. If the only reason that somebody risked his life to save a drowning child who fell into Lake Michigan was really that he didn't risk his life – because he was a great swimmer, and he happened to know the child in question was the only child of a billionaire – what he thought he was doing was getting pretty good odds that somebody would give him a lot of money. The whole act feels different from the way it feels if somebody who couldn't swim too well actually did leap into Lake Michigan in order to save this child.

Yeah, there are people like that, and some of them are admirable: people who are upset by the fact that lots of people don't have enough to eat and lots of people are treated badly and some people never learn to read. This moves them so much that if they can do anything at all, they have to address this question. Hopefully or not, these people often appear kind of saintly. Although in the case of the most famous example of this, I have my doubts. That is Mother Teresa: I'm not so sure what moved that lady.

The problem with Mother Teresa is that it's not clear that she brought a whole lot of material comfort to these people, cured any diseases. That she got anybody a job. She got them to convert, so they would die in the bosom of the Savior. I'm not sure that that's enough. In some cases, it doesn't matter what the motive is. You just want people to do what it is that you think ought to be done. Surely, the old idea that what we really want is for people to do the right thing for the right reason, that makes sense. Even in a capitalist country.

DAVID BLOOM: Our educational system and standardized testing instill conformity in students. Looking at education in America in the 1800s, teaching was greatly influenced by the Germans, who taught students to be obedient. Education, in my opinion, has fought against individuality and thus against the soul. In order to maintain order in society, education has a job, and that is to teach students to obey cultural mandates.

ANDREA COSNOWSKY: But we have to be careful. Is it education that's fought against the soul, or is it obedience that has fought against the soul? I believe education at its highest level enables a person to learn how to think for themselves, but that's very dangerous in a society. If you have a society full of thinkers, you can't control the way society is going to go. It's very threatening to think.

BOB WILLEMS: One of the clients that I have right now is a charter school here in Chicago. They work with kids who are in impoverished areas. These kids have no access to education outside the public school system. They provide them education for no cost, since it is the same as going to public school. They just have a radically different approach. They get kids to go to classroom, seven in the morning until five o'clock, Monday through Friday. They get kids in for almost the same amount of hours on Saturdays. Half of their summer they are in there as well.

We know that education has to improve in very specific ways. Not just kids have to test better, but kids have to embrace that they are empowered as individuals to determine what their lives are going to be like. Huge thought, you know. But what does it take to get that instilled in kids?

It takes a lot of effort, particularly when you are starting out with kids whose education has been just on the basics. The great thing is that it succeeds. It works. Not only because the program works and because the way of educating kids works, but because the family members of these kids realize what this is about. They get it. They are not particularly educated themselves. They don't have a high academic vision of what a better education of their kids is going to be like. But they get the idea that kids are going to figure out what they are going to do with their lives and how to determine their own futures, and how to pursue life in their own way.

Schools and early education have to enforce this idea of individuality. It's a very difficult thing to do. It requires hard work and a rigorous approach by educators and the family to raise a kid that thinks individually and thinks critically about what is going in society. It is a huge task because everything else in their lives says this other thing: TV says this. Their friends say this. Their teacher says this, whatever, and you are promoting this radical idea which is: In order to accept everything that is handed to you, you got to think about things differently. Let's try this different approach.

*One looks back with appreciation to the brilliant teachers,
but with gratitude to those who touched our human feelings.
The curriculum is so much necessary raw material, but warmth is the
vital element for the growing plant and for the soul of the child.*

-Carl Jung

DAVID BLOOM: Ross Perot said the money you spend in education for kids will be the cheapest money you ever spent. But how do you relate to adult students?

WENDY CLINARD: The relationship between myself and the students here? They vary. Some of my students are on really long-term apprenticeships where they have been around upward to ten years. Others just come for classes. But I would say even if a student is coming in as a hobby,

I'm still the same exact teacher. You're close to them. If you just do this, you're all the way. That moment of change is going to happen. I love it. It doesn't matter if you're doing it once a week or if you're doing it like a hundred times a week. This is it. You decided this is what you want to do. So I'm pretty much neutral that way. Everybody gets the same excitement, teaching.

DAVID BLOOM: Same for me. So it's just a matter of what does this particular person want – and if you can provide value.

WENDY CLINARD: I've tried to guide the relationship sometimes – meaning that if I really feel like they want something different, I suggest they try. This is a love affair and it goes on to infinity. It's just as the artist, Chuck Close, says, "Inspiration is for amateurs." You do this thing over and over, and you try to preserve that first excitement that you had from it. You look for that all the time. If you become an elder in your craft, then you're looking to try to inspire your community: people that are showing up for class.

DAVID BLOOM: Where did you first find inspiration?

OSCAR BROWN, JR.: The Communist Party, my participation in that was like joining church. The people I met were too numerous to mention. There were people at all ages and stages who were influential. We were serious people, and we felt we were doing good. We certainly didn't feel like we were betraying the country. We felt that the capitalist system was betraying the interests of the majority of the people. We were trying to liberate the country from that influence. We felt that this was a good thing to do. That led us to taking all kinds of positions about women's rights and civil liberties and the rights of workers and political action. A lot of things that have happened that now are doctrine – commonplace – were considered radical in those days. I was a true believer. I wanted to be a scientific socialist. I read some of the philosophers. I read Stalin and Mao Zedong, of course; Zhdanov and others. Marx and Engels, who were philosophers and thinkers. I was searching, actually searching – but thinking I had found the answer. I was quite a zealot.

DON MEADE: I remember the Communists coming in, getting on park benches. And they had a solution: They'd go down to city hall, and they would get a list of all people that were going to be evicted. And they would pay your rent for you, and they would tell you, "We have a meeting at a school house on Friday night." You didn't show up for the meeting, they sent goons out after you, and they were worse than the system you're protesting.

OSCAR BROWN, JR.: I came to see how a few people could manipulate a whole lot of people. We would go to a meeting and decide that – in connection with the negotiations that were going on at some big company – they needed to have a work stoppage or mass rally. Two months later, what we had said we were going to do would be accomplished. It would be accomplished as a result of what half a dozen people wanted to do. Half a dozen determined and 'know what they're doing' can really maneuver among people who are just there, without any hidden agenda whatsoever.

DAVID BLOOM: What made you leave the Party?

OSCAR BROWN, JR.: Bit by bit I became disenchanted with the leadership. We had racial differences. We were always saying, "Negro and White unite to fight." Yet I never found a neighborhood in which race didn't make a difference, a big difference. I began to feel that it was necessary for the Negro people to get themselves together, because nobody wanted to unite with a cripple. We had to get our act together, and this put me in contention with some of the doctrine that was espoused by the Party at that time. I wound up writing critical stuff about it and finally getting kicked out.

DAVID BLOOM: How long did you belong?

OSCAR BROWN, JR.: Ten years, ten years. I joined when I was twenty, and I left when I was about thirty. They kicked me out of the Army for being a Communist – although they knew I was a Communist when they took me in. That was why they took me in the Army, in order to kick me out and expunge my political record. In my career as a candidate for elected office, I had run not only for the State Legislature but for Congress too. What they did was correct as a barrel of fish hooks, but that's what was going on at the time.

DON MEADE: I remember being really, really impressed with Oscar Brown's Washington trip when he did "Brother Where Are You? I know you came this way." Oh, that's powerful. We're still looking for brother. We're still looking for that brotherhood, that camaraderie, that sense of community. It's everything, because a sense of community is a sense of strength. I don't think we have that now. In fact, I'm almost sure. There are communities, but they don't function as a community. There are too many elements that prevent that now.

DAVID BLOOM: Do you think politics can ever bring people together?

TED COHEN: Politics is partly a matter of being able to hurt your enemies, help your friends, remain secure, and take care of your citizens. The United States has been terrific at that. I don't believe in special, moral knowledge. I believe in all kinds of things but not that. Thomas Jefferson says, "State a moral problem to a plowman and a professor. The plowman will give just as good an answer – and maybe a better one – because he doesn't have a whole bunch of theories." There's no more reason to think a philosopher could tell you what the right thing to do is than to think that he could tell you what the wrong thing to do is. Human beings can do that. I don't think philosophy ought to dictate behavior.

DAVID BLOOM: What about when people break laws and go before a judge?

BLANCHE MANNING: Many things happen in courtrooms that are soulful. I consider soulfulness to relate to spirituality and emotions. You can imagine how emotional proceedings are in a courtroom. Not just criminal cases but in civil cases as well, because everybody has a stake in what's happening.

DAVID BLOOM: Do you believe the adversarial process often depersonalizes the actual people on trial, that it becomes almost a high-level game between the prosecutor and the defender?

BLANCHE MANNING: It can if you let it. I think in that connection it's very important that you have an impartial arbiter – which is the judge. Let's face it, a prosecutor, for probably the wrong reasons, wants to win all their cases, and a defense attorney wants to win all of their cases. Many times, one or the other is not entitled to win, because the facts are simply not there for them to win. I think it's important that a judge have perfect control over his or her courtroom and make sure that the adversarial process is a fair process. The court has to have the sensitivity to everybody's feelings.

DAVID BLOOM: What discretion does a judge have in determining sentences for criminal activities?

BLANCHE MANNING: In 1984, the United States Sentencing Commission promulgated the guidelines which provide, basically, a grid for judges to use in imposing sentences in criminal cases and in the federal system. You look at the criminal history category of a person and you look at what the offense level is. For instance, if you sold narcotics and you sold between five to twenty kilograms, it might provide for a particular number; or if it's one to five kilograms, it provides for a lower number. It's very mechanical. The purpose of it was to eliminate the disparity in sentencing that had been going on prior to that.

For instance, you might have a judge who might be extremely sympathetic or emotional or soulful who might impose a lesser sentence on a person who had the same numbers as a person who was before a judge who didn't care. That person before the soulful judge might get ten months in jail, and the person before the judge who didn't care might get thirty years, depending on what the statute provided for. That's why they came up with the sentencing guidelines. It's taken a lot of discretion away from judges. Probably the positive aspect of that is people who commit similar crimes and have similar records get the same kind of sentence. On the other hand, there might be other mitigating factors that a court might want to take into consideration, especially if that court had a little soul.

DAVID BLOOM: Let's talk about laws. For example, I personally believe that some of the drug laws are classist and racist, and therefore unsoulful. What do you think?

BLANCHE MANNING: There has been a lot of criticism about that very issue. It pertains primarily to crack cocaine. There are very stringent sentences for possession and distribution of crack cocaine, maybe more so than for powder cocaine. It's been said that many of the arrests that are made for crack cocaine are made in minority communities and consequently that it is racist. I'm not sure that there have been any studies that have substantiated that.

That's where the sentencing guidelines come in, again, because what happens is the court has little discretion. If a court wanted to listen to this case and decide "I don't think it's any worse for this young man to have possessed the crack cocaine than it would have been had it been powder cocaine. I'm going to give him a lesser sentence." Well, you can't do that, because the sentencing guidelines provide for a certain range of imprisonment. To that extent, it certainly does appear that it might be unfair.

DAVID BLOOM: I think if you look at powder cocaine, that's an upscale drug. It's a party favor.

BLANCHE MANNING: You have to have money to purchase it, whereas crack cocaine is much cheaper.

DAVID BLOOM: Hopefully the legal system is about providing justice. How does it affect you if you have to execute laws that you find to be patently unsoulful?

BLANCHE MANNING: I think you can look to mitigating factors. You don't necessarily have to follow the sentencing guidelines if it is brought to your attention that there's some factor that is mitigating. Just as an example, a woman who has ten kids might be before the court on some kind of fraud charge. The sentencing guidelines might provide for a certain penalty, and what you are allowed to look at would be the circumstances that her kids will endure if she is imprisoned. Let's say that the range of imprisonment is twenty to thirty months; you take into account the circumstances. Ten children, no father, they'll all go to separate foster homes. Some of them have emotional problems. They need the mother. There are no relatives to care for them. These are all mitigating factors that a court can take into consideration if that court has any sensitivity to family circumstances.

When you are considering other people and their circumstances, you are looking at the other as opposed to yourself. In fact, I think in the judicial system, that's what basically happens. It's not really you that you're concerned about. When you imposed a stringent sentence on a young man that you feel had some kind of potential who just didn't use it, it's not you that you're thinking about when you emote about it. It's the young man or the young man's family. But your hands are tied with the sentencing guidelines to some extent, and as a judge you're sworn to uphold the law. You have to apply the law as it's set forth. As the high courts have said it is.

DAVID BLOOM: In a certain way, the buck stops with the jury, but then the buck stops with you. If you're dead set – in terms of your own humanity and spirituality or soulfulness – against something that you have to execute, that's a tough situation.

BLANCHE MANNING: It's heart tugging.

SOUL ON EARTH

Johann Walter Bantz

Participants in this chapter observe how other countries are different from home. Every nation has a unique character, a unique soul. Cities, neighborhoods and tribal enclaves (whether they are American suburbs or countries in the developing world) exude unique auras. Levels of soulfulness ebb and flow from region to region and era to era.

In the past, the United States has gone through many soulful periods. The Great Depression was one, the two World Wars were others – at least on the home front. All of these were times of hardship, when people voluntarily banded together to fight poverty or the Axis powers. After World War II, people say, America became too selfish for soul. We transformed ourselves into a culture of celebrity, grew increasingly fearful after 9/11, and compensated for our loss of soulfulness with growing religiosity.

In other countries, as some interviewees relate, America has been either disparaged or ignored. For example, Europeans might find us parochial and greedy. Raising their children communally and guiding them into adulthood via rituals, many Africans find us isolated. In Nepal, a pastoral lifestyle contrasts with the urban values of the Western world. In Cuba, faced with material shortages, people connect for mutual aid. However, soulfulness is not determined by class, gender or race; it can be found in any society – regardless of affluence or poverty, political repression or freedom.

Recently, the United States has been experiencing significant changes in its soul – as has much of the world. The speed of life has increased dramatically with the spread of television and the internet. We need more time to nourish our souls, but finding those moments has become difficult. We run the risk of destroying (or at least, damaging) our very civilization. Our Founding Fathers would probably look aghast at the conflict occurring between capitalism and the natural world. Yet change is inevitable – and never-ending.

Nelson Mandela — Jeremy Sutton-Hibbert

THE SOUL OF NATIONS

Culture makes people understand each other better. And if they understand each other better in their soul, it is easier to overcome the economic and political barriers. But first they have to understand that their neighbor is, in the end, just like them, with the same problems, the same questions.

-Paulo Coelho

BILL KURTIS: In the late 1800s immigrants began to sweep across America; it was the largest pastoral migration in history. They wanted free land. And they all came as Germans and Poles and Irish and Scots and Norwegians. When they hit the great plains, however, they changed into Americans. But they kept certain individual traits. Now that is beginning to go – and I think it's a shame.

NATALIJA NOGULICH: America has a beautiful soul. It came in with a soul when it was born, a nation dedicated to freedom. We paid a great price to divorce ourselves as a colony, to not be told what to do by a king. Talk about high tuition.

I love this country. My parents came from another country, and my grandfather received the Congressional Medal of Honor because he believed in what it stood for, which is freedom. So I'll walk my talk; I'll shed blood to be free. Yeah, America's got a ton of soul.

DON MEADE: I've seen some soulful times. This doesn't happen to be one of them. This is a time of transition. Transition, changing of the guard. Change is inevitable. It's always happening. Some we like, some we don't like, but it's the hardest thing to adjust to, I'll tell you that. If you got what you want, you're cozy. There is always resistance to change. So no, these are not soulful times.

CLIFF COLNOT: America has never been soulful, and – with the exception of an anomalous period from the late 1950s through the late 1960s – I have no reason to believe that it ever will be. There always were, and there always will be, pockets of soulfulness, but the notion that we're on the verge of another soulful cycle is not one that I would support or agree with. The culture and society at large is so self-centered, so narcissistic and egocentric that I would say this period of time is the nadir of soulfulness.

ANDREA COSNOWSKY: When you talk about if the soul of the country has changed, I believe that the soul has actually stayed the same. We mistake, sometimes, religious fervor for soul and emotionalism. I think the pendulum swings, and then it swings back. Our behavior was very affected by the events of 9/11. We've seen the country become reactive instead of proactive and – on some level – more frightened. We see a rise in religious activity, but that's not necessarily soul.

ELSA MORA: This is a celebrity culture. You always have the dream that maybe sometime in the future, somehow, you'll become somebody. And it is very funny, because that happens at any level. People have that dream, it's all about that big dream, because that's the essence of what we are.

TED COHEN: There are so many things wrong with the United States, we don't have enough digits in this room to count them, but by any sensible measure the United States is a fabulous success. You may worry about the abstract. It's not a very just country. It's so and so. Yeah, all right. Show me what country is.

BILL KURTIS: Almost everywhere is more soulful than the United States – or other major urban areas. And the reason is they're still pastoral. They're farmers, they're of the land, and they read the skies when they get up in the morning. They work with animals, so they respect them, because their lives depend on it.

For example, Nepal. They have no roads in Nepal outside of Katmandu. You have to walk. They don't even have horses up around ten thousand feet. Or carts. So everywhere you go you carry all of your goods. We could never make it if we didn't have somebody carry the packs. The interstate highway is about this wide. It runs through backyards and through very steep slopes. And people are friendly as you go by. You're looking right into their lives and they're looking back. It's the most wonderful feeling because you're being invited into the life of a village. It's like living in the Middle Ages.

I can see it right now: They were pounding metal into a knife. There were little stone bridges over the water that came down from the steep slopes. They would channel that water into little mills that would give them grinding power. It was like the land of the hobbits that was real. And they had their own religion. They believe in a creation myth that their god, or the first of their race, came from the forest in a cave. They can see it and look at it. There's something simple and beautiful about that.

ELSA MORA: I feel very fortunate, because I had the opportunity of living in two different places: Cuba and the United States. So I can now see very clearly the differences between living in the kind of place where you don't have any kind of material things and living on the other side where you have everything. It's very contradictory, because you think, "Well, after I have everything, all the material things, it's going to be even better for me because now I can do whatever I want." In the end you realize art, all the things you create as an artist, they don't have anything to do with material things. It's all about human connections.

For example, in Cuba, in poor countries in general, there aren't many obstacles between you and other people. It's easier to connect with people. You walk on the street, and it's easier to talk with people. You are waiting for the bus, and in two seconds, you start talking with somebody, and you tell that person the story of your life. That person tells you everything. Then you won't see that person anymore, but you feel great – like wow, this is like daily therapy. I get to talk with everybody.

You come to this country and it's so much the opposite. People are afraid. You can't just go on the street and say, "Hey. Hello. How are you? Let's talk." They're going to think this is very crazy. I'm suspicious about this person. Why? Because there's so many things between any person on the street and me. There are many fears. There are many things that make you feel uncomfortable. It's better to be careful. It takes longer to have friends. It takes longer to connect with everything.

BILL HORBERG: It was very life-altering for me to be in third world countries, to be in countries where English wasn't the first or primary language, to be responsible for the management of some large-scale projects involving international and multinational crews, for getting exposed to different styles and personalities that come from different cultures and how they cooperate or communicate or work in groups – or fail to work easily in groups. I think that was a big part of what led me to find and discover my wife, Elsa, having been to Vietnam and Cuba and Romania and other far-off parts of the world. It really opened my mind to different people from different cultures.

ELSA MORA: Soul is around that idea about connecting with people on many levels. It doesn't have to be even personal. It's just about knowing there is something around you that is easy for you to live with. That's why when you go to a country like Cuba, for example, as soon as you arrive in the airport, you can smell that in the air. People are so relaxed. Okay, they don't have anything, but that's a good thing. When you have too much, it's hard to keep looking for connection.

When I came here in the beginning, I couldn't speak any English, and that was hard. On some level that was great, because I couldn't understand a word, so I had to be more focused on something else: on the way people get together, how they talk and use their body language, and I was very curious. Wow, here when you meet somebody, you don't hug that person and you don't kiss that person. That is kind of crazy. It's like, let's keep the distance and maybe later when I feel more comfortable that will happen.

In Cuba, as soon as you meet somebody, "Hello. How are you?" Kisses, because you're not afraid. It's something really, and all that experience has a lot to do with making it easier for you to develop a creative world, because creation has a lot to do with experiences. You experience more the human side of life. Here you experience more the material side of life, and all the material experiences are very superficial. It's the kind of pleasure you feel for a little while – and then it's gone. It doesn't stay in your interior world the same way as a human experience.

In Cuba, for example, when I traveled from the province where I was living to Havana, it was horrible. Here you take a bus or whatever. There that was like one week waiting for a bus to go. Then we had to wait in the terminal, many people, but after two days, you were part of a big community. Every kind of person was there: doctors, artists, students, old people, young people, black people, white people. That was great. I was suffering, because I just want to go to Havana, I need to go there, but in some way I'm fine. I'm having fun. I'm talking and laughing. I don't have food, but somebody else has a banana, something he is giving to me, so that's priceless. You feel alive. Of course I didn't know that was so special until now when I don't have that every day in my life.

BILL KURTIS: I fell in love with Africa. Primarily because it looks like you should be there. Isak Dinesen said that the elephants were moving slowly as if they had an appointment at the end of the world. You do feel like you're part of them. Very quickly you get into their rhythm. And the people are welcoming and open. I spent time with the Maasai, and they're just the most giving and generous. There is an honesty there that you share everything. Why? Because you don't have anything. Wealth is cattle. Your status symbol is having more cattle than anyone else.

The young men are circumcised when they are sixteen and sent away for seven years. And I said, "Why send them away for seven years?" They said, "Well, they learn how to take care of the cattle and how to sustain themselves. And they learn how to be adults." I said, "Oh, that's not a bad idea." They are trained in how to find roots, how to hunt, where the animals are, how to track and find spoor. It's remarkable, and they take it very seriously. But as part of all this, there is a transition, a passage. A natural passage and tests to become a man. So they feel pride in that.

They are shaped into the army of the Maasai so they can fight, into a band of brothers that they will grow with through their lives. They elect a chief and a shaman and assistants. Each has a role in the village. And they go and respect elders to lead and make decisions until they take their place. Then they come back to the village and enter as elders. They are given cattle and they start their own life and get married. All the time, their age group ascends through the village. It's very simple and easy to see. I'm sure they have thieves and characters that don't live up to the expectations of the elders, but they take care in training and raising. It takes a village of their young people.

I think we can learn some things from them rather than know it all and take our way of living to everybody else. Given the choice, they'd probably be here. They would like to wear Western clothes. They certainly would like all the little conveniences that make life easier and more pleasurable. But they don't know how good they have it.

DAVID BLOOM: Do you think that America has much allure for people in other countries?

TED COHEN: There's so much difficulty that Europeans – particularly the French but also the Germans – have because of America. They resent us. They envy us. They think that we ought to listen to them, because they're older and wiser. We don't seem to do that. France even less than England can't grasp the idea that they don't matter much anymore. They don't. It's all happened pretty quickly. Of course, what they really can't quite grasp is the fact that it is their own fault.

I'm inclined to believe a view of a friend of mine named Charles Lipson who is a political scientist. He says that in the next century people will have some difficulty understanding why in the twentieth century there were two world wars. It's going to look clear to them that there was one world war which had a certain cessation and then started up again. Maybe the second part of it had racial features that the first part hadn't, but something started in 1914 and didn't end until 1945. By the time it was over, tens of millions of people had been killed. Economies had been ruined, and generations had been lost. That's something that these very sophisticated Europeans did to themselves. It's one of the reasons why I pay no attention.

I am not moved in the least by what Europeans think about why we invaded Iraq. In my view, the French have always fought when they shouldn't have, never fought when they should have. Why would you listen to them? These are the people who, once Germany had been defeated in 1918, somehow let it all start up again. I'm amazed by that. And it's a real old story, this French attitude of condescension toward the United States. It's wonderful to read the one person who wasn't going to put up with any of that crap. That's Mark Twain. He's saying that around 1900... But they are wonderful places to visit.

DAVID BLOOM: Well, as we've learned in the history of America, a lot of virtue lies in who's got the power. When you've got the power, that makes you virtuous right now. As far as I'm concerned, that's part of the problem of America. The arrogance is just dripping.

BILL HORBERG: Often in America what we see and view of the world is parochial and filtered through our limited curiosity or limited access to the truths about other people in other cultures. I'm just a kid from the streets of Chicago, but sometimes the world would come to Chicago. I've always tried to have a very outward posture towards the whole world and wanted to look beyond the borders of my experience of my neighborhood, of my city, of my family, of my religion, and really get out into a deeper explanation of the Earth that we're on and the people that are on it and the multifarious and multicolored shades of human experience that are out there.

CLIFF COLNOT: In a larger sense of the word, soul is not referenced by any specific variable – whether it be region, nation, culture, religion, gender, age, class. It cuts across all those variables.

DON MEADE: I respect cultures because I do believe that it's not imperative that one speaks the language that well. It is imperative that we respect their culture. And, if we respect their culture, they will give you a pass on misspelled words or misspelled meanings. They will help you along, they will further you on and straighten out the meaning of things. But when you have a total disregard for a culture…

BOB WILLEMS: The rest of the world looks at the United States and thinks that there are a lot of things that we do as a society and as a culture that have huge implications on other countries. We, as members of the society, don't really think very carefully about that, generally speaking. People have to have individual consciousness. They have to think more broadly about what are the values of the society. How do we go about finding that? If there is a soul to our country, what is that soul? And how do I get other people on board to start asking that question with me? Yes, I don't think that our culture or society can realize broader visions of what they want to be without concerning itself with these questions.

DAVID BLOOM: It's ironic that in the Great Depression, when people had nothing to speak of, they were full of hope.

DON MEADE: Oh yes, it was a soulful time. I mean, souls were all over the place. It was happening! Remember when Cannonball Adderley did the tune "Things Are Getting Better?" That's an acknowledgment. Survival compels you to call on your soul. Whatever that power is, whatever that force is, you're saying help, help, help! You know, everybody had a long coat on, everybody was lined up to get whatever was being passed out that day. Everybody had a Hoover blanket over their arm. You know what a "Hoover blanket" was?

DAVID BLOOM: No.

DON MEADE: A newspaper. It was a Herald Examiner then, or a Tribune. You took the newspaper, you opened it up. It said "Worse, Worse, and Worse." And you took the newspaper to the park, and you put it over your face and behind your head, and you went to sleep. It was your blanket. Remember that. A newspaper during the Depression was a blanket.

DAVID BLOOM: In that period, how did people treat each other? Did they help one another?

DON MEADE: We all had one thing in common: most of us were poor. Out of work, displaced, future very bleak, no end in sight. But it was a kinder time. People were searching the soul. They were looking and seeing this guy was no better or no worse than me.

I remember when I was a kid, my grandfather was saying that it was the first time that you ever went to the poor house in a car. You know, it took me twenty years to figure out what he was saying. Well, if you go back to the Depression era, that time, most people had a car. One morning they woke up, they had a car but no gas. Or they had a little money, but the gas station was closed. Big signs all over the store: Bakery was closed. You couldn't get no bread or no buns. Most people were poor. That's history.

STUDS TERKEL: The '30s, the Great Depression – there was a hope and there was a feeling there, that the whole deal – not just Roosevelt – something was going to be better.

DAVID BLOOM: The 1960s were also an era of disruption and hope. Wasn't that a similarly soulful time?

STUDS TERKEL: In the '60s, there was that horrendous adventure in Vietnam, and the protests also brought forth all sorts of feelings. So those two moments were high moments, you see, of certain hope.

CLIFF COLNOT: The question of whether or not the civil rights movement in the 1960s had an effect on soul is an excellent question, and I would suggest that it depends upon which civil rights movement you're referring to. If one is referring to the Martin Luther King civil rights movement, then I would say absolutely. If one is referring to the segregationist civil rights movement which was geared towards black power and the separation of blacks and whites, then I would say absolutely not. If you're calling that the civil rights movement, it's a question of semantics, but it was certainly destructive to soul.

OSCAR BROWN, JR.: Now, when we're talking about soul, it came to represent a cultural aspect identified particularly with black people to the point where I wrote song called "The People of Soul." What I'm talking about is people of a certain spiritual outlook on life that have faith in the unseen, in the evidence of things unseen. They accept that in a sense. It certainly could be called a superstitious quality where you're just taking a whole bunch of things on faith. You hope that things are that way. So people who went through that lifestyle – the "Negro" experience of black life in America – who had those characteristics were soulful.

CLIFF COLNOT: Of course, to be soulful in the macro sense of the word has nothing to do necessarily with blacks in America, with race, with what nation you lived in or grew up in. Soulfulness is a concept and a reality for people all over the world.

DAVID BLOOM: Is soulfulness a reality for people of every age? Or do you need to reach a certain level of maturity to be soulful?

DAVE LIEBMAN: I think it's much harder now to be a young person than it was in our time. In our time, it was black or white; you are a rebel or you aren't, you join the system or you don't. Now, what is the contra system? There is no contra system. If you are part of the system, you almost have no choice because otherwise, you are going to sit on an island. There are no damn islands left. It's rough there now.

TED COHEN: There's a book which in my opinion is really a bad book, but it was enormously successful: *The Closing of the American Mind*. It was written by a former colleague of mine, now dead, Allen Bloom. There's a section in which he really shows you there's something he deeply doesn't understand. He writes about the music that young people listen to, and he doesn't like it at all. He thinks there's something wrong with these young people. What he doesn't understand is that not only was that music not meant to appeal to him, it was absolutely meant not to appeal to him. That was part of its point. He just doesn't get it.

DON MEADE: So what's the difference? What do you subscribe to? What do you know about your existence.? How well have you tracked yourself and paced yourself? That depends on what you know, who to believe, what not to believe. That's all part of that mix. Because if somebody else tells you, they're going to tell you what they want to tell you. Ma and Pa and Grandma and Grandpa can teach you only so much.

What did life teach you after you left home? That's the important thing. If you don't believe it, graduate from college then go to IBM, or Xerox or one of them. First thing they do is shake your hand and say congratulations on being a valedictorian or however you come out. Take that diploma home, show up Monday morning and we're going to teach you the IBM way. School's never out – ever! Nobody ever graduates. It's just one phase to another one. It's an escalated process, life. Your job, technology, change, transition, all this is part of one mix. And that's what we learn in life.

TOM BURRELL: I have noticed a change in the soul aura in the country. As we have become more profit-oriented, as we have become more mechanized, industrialized, computerized, there has been a lessening of individuality and a lessening, therefore, of individual introspection, and there has been an increase in fear and fearfulness, an increase in greed. It's scary. So I think one of the things that really has struck me over the past twenty-five years is how people have changed. Something has happened in the psyche of our nation that's caused people just to behave differently. I mean, what happened?

BILL KURTIS: We live in a homogenized nation. The soul of America is lost and its individuality, its character. Everybody wants a strip mall that looks like the one outside Indianapolis. Everybody wants a Walmart outside town because that marks success. We've lost the character of our old buildings; we tear them down. It's very difficult even to find accents in different parts of the country. They were so nifty. I heard a Cajun accent down in New Orleans a week or so ago, and I wanted to follow him around and just listen to the guy talk. So we're not distinguishing between us. Television has done it.

TOM BURRELL: I was just 13, I think about 13, when TV started to come in. There was one TV on the block, about 1952, maybe 1951. They first came out maybe 1948, 1949, but on our block it was later. At that time TV was not a distraction away from social interaction; it was a thing that lubricated social interaction because everybody got together to watch television. To watch the Al Benson show, to watch roller derby, to watch wrestling, Gorgeous George. You know, it was a thing. But I do believe that television kind of got the ball rolling towards lack of human social interaction, because it spawned other things as well, the computer and so forth. I think the computer is the ultimate right now, in terms of taking people away from each other.

Powpow Native-American

HIGH-TECH SOUL

The devil has put a penalty on all things we enjoy in life.
Either we suffer in health or we suffer in soul or we get fat.

-Albert Einstein

DON MEADE: Technology will be a hindrance. It will probably take us farther away. Okay? Remember Newton Minow saying that television is a vast wasteland. In so many ways, he probably was right. Too many voices. Somebody's got to hold still while somebody talks. We have to have a will. Hope is eternal. Okay? Hope is always imminent. You buy a lottery ticket for a dollar, you buy a dollar's worth of hope. Hope is always right around the corner. All we have to do is ask it to come around. And hope, don't mean it's going to happen. But it's that thing that keeps us going.

DAVE LIEBMAN: Technology is happening just too fast for the human mind to cope with: medical, genetics, everything. Plus all the crazy shit that they can do now. We are in another industrial revolution that's so obvious and so apparent because we see it every minute. At the same time, technology is dumbing down the people. You are not going to say no to the phone. You need it. But with the computerization of the world and the whole way it's moving, it's hard to be positive and find a way through.

Now, in the third world they're just glad to have choices. We are really talking about context here. We can say, "We don't need this anymore." But if you live in Tanganyika, you are glad that you have a refrigerator. It's really contextual. Everything is happening at the same time now.

BOB WILLEMS: Technology is a tool just like any other tool that has been created by mankind since people rubbed sticks together to come up with fire. I've worked with nonprofit organizations who have tremendous ideas for what they want to do, and they are visionary and passionate people. They have given profound thought to how they want to make the world a different place. When they come to me with the idea that technology is going to be some watershed thing, it's usually a sign that they need a little work with their thinking.

I'm most inspired by organizations that have very broad visions as to what they want to achieve, and they're not unwilling to commit the hard work it takes to hone that internal plan – not just a great idea. You want to have a website, you want to have a teleconference, all this great stuff. You have a real vision for that: Here's what we're going to do, here's a map for the future of what we want to do for our agenda and how we want to change the world.

You can instantly reach very wide audiences and touch people through stories: what your mission is, what your agenda is all about. It can be a huge, enabling thing for somebody who has a great idea but not a lot of funding. They can instantly reach the world, at least the online world, although it can't make up for deficiencies that are there offline. Again, one of the great things that I see in my work is that the internet, in particular, gives people a medium to communicate these types of ideas on a very large scale without having a lot of resources.

For example, I think campaign finance performance is an issue, because basically for everybody who's in the office right now, their campaigns have been bought and paid for by people with huge financial interests. Twenty years ago, to get that voice amplified to the point where thousands or hundreds of thousands of people were listening to it, I really had to have a priesthood of an organization behind me. I had to be printing newsletters and find a way to get this message out on a big scale to the world.

Right now I can create a webpage, and I can find other people with similar ideas on the internet and exchange ideas and encourage people who my message resonates with to go check out other things. I think there is empathy for change in society right now. This technology boom gives a voice to people who think more individually or question things in society, who have ideas that are not popular, that are not money makers, that aren't going to get somebody rich or famous, but they will ultimately change the world.

DAVID BLOOM: In a certain way the internet is the last hope for individuality and for sharing. Do you think the internet also has its challenges?

BOB WILLEMS: Yes. I think the internet represents a threat in the same way that any vehicle or tool for dissent represents a threat. The same analogy for broadcast media. The airwaves are owned by the public. You and I have as much claim on the frequency that CBS is broadcast on as does CBS. We lease these airwaves to these huge corporations, and we specifically say this is for the good of the people. The internet runs the same risk. It has such an enabling power to it. It is such a democratizing force in some ways. But the political structure gets in there and starts to try and make decisions: Things are going to be this way but not that way. You can share things this way but you can't share things in this way. It's already chipping away at the block. I think the good thing is at its core, the design of the thing, you can't take it apart and segment it. It's a network. It's a connection between individuals in a very significant way.

ANDREA COSNOWSKY: Technology could be good in and of itself in that it supposedly was going to – once upon a time – make our lives easier. It's made us able to do more in a shorter amount of time so that we can get more done. We've lost sight of what technology was supposed to do, which was to give us more time to be with our families and even to be with ourselves.

I like the idea of Shabbat: taking a day of rest where I don't have access to my computer and the internet, and I don't turn on music. I have a day of quiet, and I am with my family. I don't have to be anywhere because I have to have downtime. It's called down because I'm not up and running, and I'm not hooked up or online; it's down, I'm down. Yet from that time of reflection and rest, I have enough energy to take the next six days with more vigor than I would if I hadn't taken a day off to be with my family and to be with myself. It's sort of like recharging our batteries.

This idea of technology, we can say technology is bad. Oh, look at what it's done to our society, but I think it is we who have been irresponsible. We haven't insisted that we take time back from the technology. We can utilize technology for its purpose, which is to give us the opportunity to do more, but we have to remember as a soul, souls need to be nourished as well. If we don't nourish our soul, it will wither.

BILL KURTIS: We keep inventing things to make life easier, to give us more pleasure. From television we entertain ourselves, and we don't want a minute of our day to be boring, without some pleasure or gratification or stimulation or satisfaction. I think we're like hamsters – running so fast that we've lost touch with the value of the world in which we live.

ANDREA COSNOWSKY: What is the new normative? It's coffee. It's these caffeinated drinks. They're marketing them to children now. We are trying to keep up, and we're using outside means. It'll be interesting to see what effect it has on our souls, but as our bodies mutate – survival of the fittest – we'll see what happens. Maybe there's something about our souls that we haven't realized, that this is just the next direction.

Shibuya Crossing, Tokyo   Timo Volz

THE SPEED OF SOUL

I put my heart and my soul into my work, and have lost my mind in the process.

-Vincent Van Gogh

BILL KURTIS: I think you could say that the speed of life has come to the point where it has diminished soulfulness. We like things fast. There's even a book out called *Blink*. That first impulse. Television programming: advertising is reduced to one minute. Stories have been condensed to under thirty seconds, ten seconds if possible. Headline services. That's all you want; that's all we appear to have time for. And one of the reasons is that we're catching it on the run. Now we have video that comes over our cell phones. Where do you spend most of your time eating? At a fast food – fast because you don't sit down and enjoy it. At a Starbuck's because you can grab it and go with a little plastic cap on the top. Our lives have been speeded up to the point where we don't spend any time with ourselves. So how can we know who we are if we never let the brain waves work?

We've filled our lives with tools – electronic tools – to get to work faster, to communicate faster. You lose that personal time. We've speeded our lives up, which means that we have lost the real value of appreciating the life around us. How many people say, "Was that last year or five years ago?" Time goes so fast. I was visiting my daughter in San Francisco and she said, "I've been here eighteen years." I said, "Eighteen years? You just graduated!"

Where does it go? It's the blink of an eye. If you were forced to wait for spring before doing things – or for the harvest next fall – then you would have all that time in between to appreciate life.

TOM BURRELL: It's amazing how things have changed. You want to resist the temptation of being an old fogey and talking about the good ol' days and everything being relative and everybody thought the same thing and so forth, but I believe there's been some significant, measurable, quantifiable kinds of eruptions in our society.

BILL KURTIS: If you look at every civilization, it has destroyed itself by exhausting its resources and not having any more to eat. Big farms – corporate farming has now taken over our food supply. Agribusiness – only two percent of our population actually grows food for the rest of us to eat. Local farmers are just not here. That trend has to be reversed. We have over-sugared, over-processed everything from meat to grains. This food is the tobacco of tomorrow, and we may be killing ourselves. Everybody senses that.

We don't look at it like a spaceship: this precious globe that exists – at least from what we can tell – nowhere else in the universe. And we're wasting it. We're melting the glaciers, we're causing the sea levels to rise, and we're getting ready to face a disaster far worse than any war: global warming. But it's hard to stop the treadmill.

BOB WILLEMS: I'm not a communist, I'm not a socialist, I'm a hopeful democrat and into the market economy. A lot of the problem lies where commerce comes into people's lives. Is it a tool for you to enable what you're going to do with your life? Or is it what your life is about? That's the thing that's wrong right now. People learn at a very early age how to be consumers way before they learn how to be individuals or how to be members of a democracy or citizens.

Citizenship is something people think about when they vote once a year, or when they see a debate on TV between presidential candidates and they think, "Who's the worst guy out there?" But decades before that, they were learning how to be consumers. They were bombarded with "You're buying this, and this will make you happy." Where's the balance in that?

I think if the founding fathers were to be beamed back into our society right now and took a look at the way things are, "This is not what we are talking about. We wanted people to be able to be self-determined economically. But we didn't want the economy to run the show." The politics, the democracy was supposed to be about the individual and being able to pursue liberty and happiness. Economic gain, that's great, but to the extent that it becomes the dominant force to the expense of other things that people can pursue in their lives, the whole thing is off-kilter. I don't see soulful expression.

DAVID BLOOM: Do you believe capitalism is antithetical to soulfulness?

CLIFF COLNOT: That's a superb line of inquiry – and very complex. I believe that the archetype of capitalism that we have been familiar with over years and years is, in fact, incompatible with soulfulness. However, I have spent a lot of time thinking about this and discussing this with various colleagues and friends. I passionately believe that if one is creative and one is soulful and one is imaginative, one can craft a personal brand of capitalism that is no way incompatible with soulfulness, that, in fact, promotes soulfulness. Is it possible for an individual to be very wealthy and at the same time be soulful? Absolutely.

BOB WILLEMS: They say America is in a better shape than any other country. In a lot of ways you can't disagree. But what I think is patently obvious is we don't invest for tomorrow. We take money and think, "What I can do by Thursday with this money?" When you grow a business, do you think, "Okay. I am going to go out and rip people off so that next week I have a big pile of money?" Or do you think, "Thirty years from now, I want to have this thing that does X, Y, or Z?" But what fosters this long-term vision when it's all about turning profit in the short term, when it's more cash, more money, money, money, money?

DAVID BLOOM: So where do you find soulfulness in America? Is there a special place that's more soulful than any other?

BILL KURTIS: Soulfulness comes from that pastoral solitude where you can connect directly with nature, because there is a link with this world where we started as human beings. It's the chlorophyll and the leaves. It's the energy that comes from the earth and the cycle of life. And there are places, regions, that are more stimulating, but it depends on who you are.

WENDY CLINARD: Where I'm from, there has always been this pull-and-tug between the natural world and this amazing urban world, where there are ideas, the arts and the humanity that make me feel alive. In the middle of the outdoors the landscape comes awake, and I feel the awe of being in a place that has those gigantic expanses.

Internally, the outdoors means a certain quality of light, a time of day. But the city does the same thing to me. You grow because you're around so many human beings with so many world views and sensibilities. It changes you if you're open for the change.

BILL KURTIS: Cities are repositories of very stimulating things. So you live in the city for the energy. It's exciting. There's a lot of places to go, people to run into, things to do. But soulful? It can be soulful, I suppose, to some. Especially if you were raised here. But not in my mind. My place is the prairie. I find a magic in it. It's seventy-five percent sky. And that bowl of blue on top of native grasses that have been growing for a long time has this wide-open potential. I can feel the energy. And nobody has to say anything to me. It just kind of rises within as I drive into it.

On my ranch in Kansas, I walk up on a little knob of a hill that I call Secret Meadow. I can stand there and feel the pulse of the earth beneath my feet and listen to the breeze going through the grasses and the birds in the trees and look up at a soaring eagle going by. And sunsets that will knock your socks off. You realize that the Indians who lived there had their own religion that was carved out of their existence, right there. It was finding God or the Great Spirit in every living thing – in the trees, in the grasses – that each had a soul.

The more we remove ourselves from that moment, the more we lose respect for the world we live in. We don't care about it. We use the world as if these resources were ours to consume and throw away. We have gotten terribly far, I think, from what is really valuable in life. I mean, do you stop and think how many times you actually set foot on real earth that isn't a manicured lawn, concrete sidewalk, asphalt street, ever? Until you get out to a public space that has been set aside and say, okay, this is real earth.

DON MEADE: It wasn't until I went into the service that I saw a mountain, I saw a bluff, I saw a few semi-hills. But I grew up in a flatland. Anything from Kansas to Ohio is all flat land. That's all I ever saw! But within the confines of that American Serengeti, that Middle America thing, I also saw an urban life. I was just forty miles from Chicago. So I had the best of both worlds: the rural world and the cosmopolitan urban lifestyle, the streets and alleys of the urban world and the hills and valleys of the rural life. The glare and glow of the neon sign.

We cried about the smokestacks in Gary, South Chicago, Pittsburg, Youngstown, Cleveland, St. Louis, all of those things. And now we're crying because they're gone. Change, it's a bittersweet thing.

SOULLESS

Hatim Belyamani

Some people are born soulful, but others need to learn – and soulfulness is not acquired cheaply. The purchase price for soul entails connecting with yourself and with others, adhering to truth, and shunning superficiality. The Devil – or whatever we call our worst instincts – loves to snap up souls wholesale, and soul-sellers end up soulless, even evil.

People interviewed here describe how good souls can become corrupted by greed and fear, as well as how people hide their souls, or fail to let them develop. Evil souls cause pain in others, partly because they endure pain themselves. Although empathy is a significant component of soulfulness, dictators gain power through their empathy with the public.

This chapter explores the conditions of soullessness and asks if evil people lack soul entirely – or if their souls are just corrupt. Because our world is too complex to be binary, human behavior manifests itself on a continuum, from the sublime to the stinky. Soulfulness employed sporadically can be an end stage on the road to infamy – or a stepping-stone to a fully realized self.

BARRETT DOSS: When I was in about seventh grade, I was best friends with this girl, and she was pretty manipulative. She would just mess around with a lot of people's minds, including mine. I had talked to my mom about how sometimes I felt like I wasn't doing things that I really wanted to be doing. Not bad things, like drinking or drugs or anything, but I was ignoring people who I hadn't ignored before. I wasn't being nice to people who had been my friends, because she was telling me not to talk to them. After I talked to my mom about it, we decided that probably the best thing to do is to just slowly cut her out of my life.

As a result, I stopped talking to her, and after about a week she came to school, and she pulled me aside. She was like, "I took sixteen Advil last night. It was because you weren't talking to me. You've hurt me. I wanted to kill myself." I panicked, and she ended up telling pretty much everybody. I mean, she told the loudmouths and, of course, word spread. I lost a lot of friends, all of my friends, or all of the people that I thought were my friends. There was a period where I didn't really have any friends in school. I didn't have anybody to talk to except for my mom and my family.

CLIFF COLNOT: There's a criterion of inclusivity for someone to be soulful. If there's an exclusion of other people by anyone, I think they've abdicated their right to be soulful. For instance, someone who might be prejudiced against black people and feel as if they are inferior to WASPs or to Caucasians would, in my opinion, be instantaneously excused from the club of soulful humans. In the same way, somebody that was anti-Semitic or homophobic or sexist or classist, I believe those political views are an anathema to soulfulness.

BARRETT DOSS: People who are being mean to other people, they probably don't look at it that way. They probably look at it that they're doing it for some other cause. They say they're doing a good thing for someone else and those other people are really the ones that are bad and what they're doing is right. You can be persuaded on what's right or wrong.

NATALIJA NOGULICH: I think our soul has been suffering in recent years. And I think it's suffering exactly the way an individual would suffer – when it is not being its true self. That's when you suffer: when you want to accommodate a falsehood around you, when you no longer are doing right for the sake of doing right. For the principle. We know what's right. We know it, a child knows it. And when we give that up and call it something else, our soul suffers.

DAVID BLOOM: When people behave in an unsoulful fashion, what's going on there?

BILL KURTIS: They have lost touch with themselves. They're not in control of their lives. We all diverge at some point. We have responsibilities of family. We want things, perhaps for a reason that we shouldn't: greed. We want to make some money. And we're doing activities that we don't particularly like. You don't have to hate it, but it's just not within your flow. It doesn't come from a love from within and, consequently, it may or may not be successful. But it's not enjoyable.

TOM BURRELL: Greed and fear, I think, are inextricably tied. The more you fear, the greedier you are; the greedier you are, the more you fear. The greedier and more fearful you are, the more callous you are about people, because you're basically trying to hold on to something out of this fear and out of this greed that makes you less considerate of other people, makes you less introspective, makes you less soulful, because you can't deal with that.

RICK KOGAN: Soul is about energy. Soul is about feeling. And there are certain people in this world, like John Wayne Gacy, who are obviously cut off from feeling. I feel bad for them. Soul, which I believe is inherent in every human being, can be corrupted. I certainly think that's true, where it becomes totally misguided, where by dint of… maybe genetics, or possibly environment, it can be taken down some kind of dark path.

DAVID BLOOM: But isn't the soul always there, even when we try to conceal it?

RICK KOGAN: All I'm saying is there is a real everybody. There is a real person. You hide it. I hide it. He hides it. They hide it. We all have to hide it, because this is conventional society. I can't go through my life telling the truth to everybody. I can't walk around naked. Nobody can go through this life being their real selves, because there's too much shit involved. It's what's made you functional in the world.

NATALIJA NOGULICH: Nobody's unsoulful in my view. But people need the awakening, the awareness. Someone who is steeped in ignorance and what we would define as, for lack of a better word, evil ways is not without soul. They're not in touch with it, and they're not acting congruent with their true nature, which I believe is good. I believe our true nature is good. But what is it then?

Well, it can be a number of things. It can be a blind following of a bad doctrine, you know? Ignorance. Ignorance can be very damaging. So we need to wake up to it – but not say that someone is without a soul and then should be eliminated. Someone breaks the law, should they be punished? Oh, yeah. You've got to have a law or you have chaos. We need to have a sense of principle. Because principle is love.

Being one with what's right is being loving. It's not being harmful or judgmental or better than. But wrong actions need to be arrested so that we can create a space for clear expression of humanity – which I think is good. I'm kind of on the positive side of things. I see good.

CHRISSY DELACOTTA: I think everyone's born with a good soul. You're innately good when you're born and when you're a baby, but as you grow older, if you find negative things in yourself, you can become bad. Certain people may be getting closer and closer to having an evil soul, but I don't think you're born with an evil soul.

VAN SANDWICK: Maybe soulfulness is in the eye of the beholder. If that person is into the same stuff that you're expressing, then you're soulful to them but maybe not someone else. Like maybe around your friends, you're acting weird to try to make yourself fit in. And then when you go home and you're with your family, you're your regular self again. Something like that can happen.

CLIFF COLNOT: I don't think it's reasonable that somebody would be selectively soulful. I'm sure you've known people who, when you see them in their family environment with their children and grandchildren, they're incredibly soulful, but that same person in business is completely avaricious and mean-spirited and abusive.

The notion that there are extenuating circumstances and contexts in which soulfulness can be suspended out because of economic and political realities is cowardly, and I do not believe that at all. I know people who are soulful every moment that they're awake, every moment that they're conscious. So I would say anybody who would posit the notion that to survive in the world one must compromise soulfulness based on the context is engaging in specious rhetoric, and I would take them to task for that.

CHARLES JAFFE: People express themselves in all kinds of ways. People are expressing ways of protecting themselves every bit as much as they're expressing what's deeply inside. You look at certain acts like a violent act – or I could turn it on its head and say, "Is the expression of generosity an expression of soulfulness?" Well, maybe yes and maybe no. It may be a combination of both. Is a person who does something good or does something bad, are they expressing their innermost being, or are they expressing some self-protection against awareness of their innermost being?

BOB WILLEMS: I think individuality has a huge role. I don't want to appear too negative about the state of society today, but people are willing to just go with the flow and get absorbed by advertising, marketing, what the consensus is. Some political figures promote some ideology, and then it's much easier to adapt and conform than it is to think independently. What do I as a person, independent of political party or organization or church, think about all these things, and what's my view on the world?

Loyalty to petrified opinion never yet broke a chain or freed a human soul.

-Mark Twain

BILL KURTIS: Ease of acquisition trumps soulfulness because it doesn't take any effort to get. It's sort of coming our way – we have input hitting us all the time and then usually have to bat it away. All you have to do is relax and in comes radio, television, movies. Television doesn't even cost anything. Music. Think of all the things that we have created to theoretically make our world a little better, right down to the iPod. On the other hand, you know, it separates us from having to confront problems we have – but also from appreciating the sunset and a blue sky.

DAVID BLOOM: So basically, you're saying that we've created an electronic elixir that buffers us from ourselves.

BILL KURTIS: Or it's a psychiatrist. It's therapy that can be pleasing, very pleasing. But in the process, it layers in these intrusions so that we don't have to face our problems or enjoy the real things, which are relationships, children, communication with the people around us. And then we ask, well, why are we breaking up?

TOM BURRELL: We don't do enough encouraging people to seek the truth, especially in today's environment. To seek the truth and to speak the truth, to seek the truth and after finding it, to speak it. I mean, nobody in public life says what they think is the truth. We are in an environment now where the rules of the game are changed, and it's Machiavellian in the sense that we have a certain objective and whatever we have to say to get there takes us further and further away from our humanity and further and further away from soulfulness. I think that it's a real threat to civilization.

BILL HORBERG: The ascendancy of celebrity culture has really put a premium on the fake and the inauthentic. I feel sad about what people who grow up within this culture are fed. What they are assimilating has very little to do with searching and seeking out – or that there's any kind of premium put on authentic experience. It's frightening to me. There's a kind of simulated nature to the pop culture that we're immersed in. Whether it's films or music or the internet or video games. We're at this moment of apotheosis of the technological ability to recreate and simulate the universe.

We live in a world that's often very divorced from what I would consider to be the most important things and most important qualities of the human experience and of life. Right now the struggle that's going on in the world we're in is very much the ascension of the corporatization of the planet. Of course, corporations don't have a soul. There's no center there. There's no there there. There's just a conglomeration that's all about the profit-seeking motive.

DAVID BLOOM: If soul is not readily available, is it costly?

DON MEADE: Oooh. It can be costly. It can be devastating. In an abstract sense, it is costly because you have to stick by your conviction. Now, if you trade off your conviction for some other belief, you betray that soul. That soul is you. Can you stand up and be accounted for?

CLIFF COLNOT: I don't think soulfulness costs anything. It's a one-way street. The person who's soulful gets a great deal from being soulful, but I don't think there's any cost to being soulful. It makes it sound as if there's some type of quid pro quo or some type of punitive arrangement or some kind of Faustian arrangement which, if I'm going to be soulful, I need to barter away something. I need to come up with something to enable myself to become soulful.

NATHAN WORCESTER: Sometimes people think of their soul not like a scoreboard but something like, "My soul is better than your soul, so that means I'm a better person." But you can be a terrible person and be soulful.

DAVID BLOOM: Freud, from what I understand, had a bad feeling about people. Then he decided he wanted to understand them. Do you believe, vis-à-vis soul, that you are a relativist regarding moral or immoral actions?

CHARLES JAFFE: It gets back to that question what's the relationship of soul to morality? Yeah, I do think that if I go by my sense of what soul is, whatever the essential human experience is, then I think it is a kind of relativistic or amoral position. I don't forget that most people think of it with a value on it. It's cool to be soulful, or if you're really hip, you're soulful. But that's only part of the human experience.

A lot of what's essential and vital and core about the human experience is pretty shitty. It's pretty stinky, and people want to turn away from that. If you think of soul as the equivalent of the full richness and uniqueness of human experience, you can't have it both ways. You can't be fully soulful with just the romantic, nice parts of it.

DON MEADE: The will to hang in there, the will to persevere, that's the working of the soul. Now to suppress that will, and to walk away and deny that will, the workings of the soul lie dormant. I believe this.

DAVID BLOOM: In your job, have you ever encountered an ugly situation which caused people to forget, even to lose, their souls?

TED COHEN: A few years ago, something happened at the university that some of the faculty were concerned about. The library had fired a whole bunch of employees, and it was feared that they had fired those employees who were trying to organize a union. The president of the university appointed a committee to look into this. The committee made its report through its chairman, a very bright guy, who said a really stupid thing. He said they had investigated and found that firing these people was consistent with the budgetary needs of the library.

The obvious question was: Couldn't they have fired other people? Why these people? He said, "We couldn't go into their heads." I said, "If you didn't think you could go into their heads, then you shouldn't have agreed to be on this committee. That was the whole question. We know what happened. What we're trying to figure out is why they did it – and if you think that you can never figure that out, you're somebody who thinks there's no difference between first degree murder, second degree murder, and manslaughter."

DAVID BLOOM: If a person has no moral criteria, does that make them soulless?

STUDS TERKEL: It depends how we interpret soul. I mean, soul-less: a person who is selfish and greedy and thinks only of himself and has contempt for the rest of mankind. I'm choosing an extreme case – well, for me not that extreme, there's a touch of that in all of us. Someone who lacks a feeling – seemingly lacks a feeling. He might have a feeling, but it's not one of fraternity or whatever it might be.

CHRISSY DELACOTTA: I think that a person who isn't soulful is somebody who chooses to not care about their spirituality or to not look for anything deeper in life. They want to skim the surface of what's actually there. They just want to live out their life and do what they're told, and that kind of soul I question. You're looking for something else. You're looking for something deeper under the surface. That's the difference between someone who's soulful and someone who's not.

DAVID BLOOM: Isn't soullessness more extreme than just living superficially?

CHARLES JAFFE: Absolutely. Sociopaths have no soul. Bad people have no soul. We usually use it as a synonym for people who do things that are unempathic or hostile or show no regard for other people. If you think about what soul is, it's the essence of somebody's humanness, whatever that may be. Then yeah, it's an expression of the depth of being human.

ELSA MORA: Every single person has a soul, but some souls never develop and stay very small: even the most crazy, bad people – if you can call them bad, because nobody is completely bad or good. Some people have a life that never allowed them to develop that side. It's just connected to how complex human nature is. It's very easy to say you can develop your soul. You can do that over the years, but it's very hard when a person is in the middle of a very difficult atmosphere, surrounded by many difficult conditions. I don't mean that if you do something bad, and you don't have a nice beautiful soul, you are evil. It's not that simple.

Everything that happens has a reason, and this has to do with the atmosphere around you, with the experiences you had to face in your life. Some people are desperate to grow up, to be better, to give more things to others, to be nice people, but the conditions are so hard that it's sometimes really impossible.

ANDREA COSNOWSKY: I believe that there's no such thing as an evil soul. Souls are pure, but our actions are evil; they affect our soul. Ultimately, the soul that was given to us is pure, and it is we – through being human – who adulterate it. We are spiritual beings having a human experience rather than human beings having a spiritual experience.

TOM BURRELL: Some people are really bad people, but I wouldn't call them evil souls. I think they are people who in most instances are sick, who in most instances have a wall between themselves and their soul, their truth. They are either ignorant and blocked off, or they blocked themselves off, or have been blocked off from seeking the truth. Very often their being blocked off has to do with values and with their being taught that there are more important things than delving into issues of soulfulness: like making money, or profitability, or even being taught that you keep score by how many people you screw up – or you screw. So it has often to do with what you are taught, what you are conditioned to, and it often has to do with being sick, with having a malady, a screw loose, whatever you want to call it, that makes people who are not innately evil do evil deeds.

BARRETT DOSS: I'm not sure if people can have an evil soul unless they really, really enjoy causing other people pain. Then that's an evil soul. But I think anybody who has an evil soul is really just an unhappy person.

JEWEL TANCY: 'Evil soul.' That's a good question. I think that is very possible. Soul is the presence or power inside of us that makes us move, that makes us feel, that makes us think. A lot of us have very different presences. Some of us have a quiet presence. Some people are, "You know, he's such a quiet soul." Or, "She's so wise. She's intelligent. Oh, she's a loving soul." So I think with that, there can be an evil soul. Unfortunately, all of us have the capacity to have an evil soul.

CHARLES JAFFE: There are evil expressions. There are evil things that people do, but the idea of an evil soul goes back to a certain philosophical position that soul exists as a separate entity and may even be divinely given. There's an implication of fundamental good and evil or Godliness or Satanliness in that. From the point of view of essential humanity, that comes in all kinds of shapes and forms. Some we like and some we don't. Even evil is an expression of someone's essence, someone's soul.

DAVID BLOOM: Can you give me some examples of evil souls?

CHRISTIAN STEINBARTH: I think being a cannibal is like a bad thing.

PHILLIP VERNA: Just basically people who want to do bad things and hurt other people.

NATHAN WORCESTER: Like Jeffrey Dahmer.

TOM BREWER: Hurting people. That's a bad soul.

DEREK CHIAMPAS: I don't think that's necessarily true because someone could be doing that on accident, so you have to say "intentionally."

CHRISSY DELACOTTA: Like some psycho.

ZACK GRAHAM: As opposed to someone who accidentally killed their mother.

VAN SANDWICK: Or pushed some guy down the stairs.

ZACK GRAHAM: Or ran them over in the driveway.

BARRETT DOSS: But then when you get to the terrorist – when they go and kill people, they think that they're honoring something, so that's what makes them happy. It's their way of being soulful.

DAVID BLOOM: What about somebody like George W. Bush? Do you think he views himself as soulful?

RICK KOGAN: Absolutely, because I think Bush's definition of soulfulness is totally cocked up! I think, in the way that the word soul – and soul itself – is repressed, at some point in one's life, whether it's through religion or not, you glom onto the concept that "Yeah, I have soul, and this is what's going to get me into heaven. I am the total religious schizophrenic. I have two personalities. One kills other people," in Bush's case, "but I still remain true, and I'm doing this for all the right reasons. You know, we all make mistakes," (very few on this kind of, like, global level), "but we all make mistakes." The responsibility of allowing others to die in your name would go a long way to diminish the real you.

STUDS TERKEL: Bush was evil, obviously, for the destruction of people other than himself. He also was loony. I mean, the question is: What is nuttiness? What is insanity? If you live in a vacuum, you have a soul, a warped one. But it's connected to the Other, capital O – and the Other, by the way, could be worshipping at a minaret in the Middle East somewhere, could be in Iran or Iraq, North Korea, all the axes of evil. Does Bush have a soul? Yeah, he's human, he has a soul. Now whether he has an understanding of others is something else. I think soul involves the awareness of others and an understanding of their rights as they see it. Without the hurting of people.

NATHAN WORCESTER: I think Bush honestly thinks that he was doing what was right for America. You can hear that in his speeches; they were written by speech writers, but they were very biblical in the language he used. He's born again, but he is going to hell.

TOM BREWER: He is pretty stupid, and he has done a lot of things wrong. But I do not know if he really meant to. I think he honestly might have been listening to others and just said, "Okay, I might as well do it."

PHILLIP VERNA: I have to disagree. Maybe some of the stuff he did he felt was his soul, his duty, and maybe his wish was to have a war with Iraq. Maybe that was his soul feeling, I don't know. Different people can judge it in different ways. People when they campaign, when they try out for political office, try to appeal to a large group so they can get the maximum number of votes. Maybe that is not how they truly feel about something, but they take that stand on it because they think it will be better for them.

NATHAN WORCESTER: I do not really think that Bush was expressing his soul. I think that he did express it at one time when he was coming out of his – I do not know what to call it – when he was supposedly doing coke and getting drunk every night. Then he found God, and he ran for president and won. I do not know if he won because of his dad or because of being soulful, but I think that he came out of it being a terrible person.

DAVID BLOOM: What about Hitler, in terms of soul? What would you say about him?

CHARLES JAFFE: Hitler and soul, there's a good challenge to the ideal of evil. In order for Hitler to be able to take a country and twist it and manipulate it and move it, he had to be deeply in tune with the minds of the people. It's been said that Hitler was a very empathic person. Empathy is really a neutral concept. It's not synonymous with doing good or saying nice things. It's purely a method of coming to know other people. He was the personification of evil, and that's usually posed as having no soul or an evil soul, but Hitler did have an inner self that he expressed in his own way.

STUDS TERKEL: Did Hitler have a soul? Well, yeah, he had a demon. What happened to this withered being, this loony, this psychotic? Does a nut have a soul? What about a homicidal maniac, a serial killer? Of course there's something there. It may be perverted – unless it's connected with another. I think that's what we're talking about: connection to the OTHER. The one who is not you.

SOUL REPAIR

James Xavier Lam

In this chapter, participants describe how a lost or damaged soul can be redeemed – given sufficient effort. Because soulfulness remains a work in progress, sometimes a single attempt is enough. At other times, complete reversals in attitude and behavior become imperative. But in most cases, repair does not happen overnight. Broken souls need therapy, nourishment, and healing before they can be restored. Knowing oneself, connecting with one's roots and with others, even prayer, are some of the necessary steps that lead to the reawakening of soulfulness.

One contributor relates how a career change enabled self-actualization. In other stories, a bigot becomes an activist, a politically conservative father shows kindness to his war-resisting son, and a drug lord diverts his followers away from crime. Rebirth happens when ego disappears, when sincerity erases the need to keep score. Deleting emotional trash allows a soul to find clarity and fulfillment.

BILL KURTIS: Not many people get in to talk to a warlord, especially one who's the second largest opium grower in the world, who is caught between China and Burma and has his own little kingdom where he grows his poppies and then ships them around the world to become heroin. He had an army of twenty thousand to protect the opium. He had his own law and television station, his own airline, his own banking, his own credit cards. I mean, just a remarkable individual.

He had not seen many Americans, and most of the people within his little kingdom had never seen an American. And yet he invited me and a crew in to do a story because he wanted to communicate to the outside. He was responsible for perhaps seventy thousand people, his people, and he said, "Drugs, they're going to come get us if we continue with drugs." So he imposed his own five-year program to change. He was trying to find these alternative sources of income to change the economy. He just came to it in his own head.

I was impressed that he was doing it from his soul. He had figured it out on his own. Nobody was forcing him. He was the leader, he was the king. And he wanted to do good – as well as stay in business and do well. But he was acting out of this parental, benevolent motivation for his people, knowing that he wasn't seen in the best light by the people of the world. And I was impressed by his honesty and by this motivation that came from within, that I would say was as close to soulfulness as anybody I've met.

CLIFF COLNOT: The question of whether or not anyone can become soulful when previously not, or fall out of soulfulness when they were previously soulful, is an excellent question. I have very strong feelings that – with the exception of congenital diseases and clinically psychopathic behavior – every human being has the capacity to be soulful. I do not believe that people are born soulful. I believe that people learn to become soulful.

The idea that someone would be born again and have an epiphany of some type and then go from being a mean-spirited, abusive, racist, anti-Semitic person to the next week – because of some dramatic event in their lives – you meet that person and you say, "My heavens, Bill, you've completely changed. You're soulful now." I don't buy that. I don't find that credible. I find it credible that someone could work at being soulful, and you could notice a metamorphosis over a period of time. I don't believe that between Saturday and Monday somebody would become soulful.

TOM BURRELL: Just paying attention and being fortunate enough to be older leads you increasingly to a greater realization of truth, and it's an evolutionary kind of process with some bumps here and there, things that give you a little bit of a jump, but it's gradual. Certainly, reaching sixty-five was a major kind of a point for me, but I don't want you to think it just happened.

The closer you get to having fewer tomorrows than yesterday, the more – if you're lucky – you get to that truth of what's important, what really is. One of the things that keeps people from getting to the quintessence is not paying attention because there is no sense of urgency. There is fear, too, that keeps people from getting to it, because they may have to make some hard decisions. You know, you make some decision early in life and you make it with a certain amount of conviction, and so to question or challenge it becomes very scary.

One of the worst things in your life is to decide things early on and say that's it, that's the way it is, and to get to a later point and think that maybe you were wrong, and maybe you made a mistake, and the reason why you don't want to fool around with that is because if you peel it back, the problem is you can't do anything about it. At least that's what you think. It's gone.

The decisions you made about your family and your life, your career, your kids, what to tell them, how to raise them: "You listen to me here, let me tell you how it is," and then to say, "Wait a minute, I told myself wrong, I told them wrong. I'm not even going to deal with it," I think that's what happens. You don't want to know, you don't want to get into that. But for me it has been a gradual kind of process where you a learn a little bit more as you go.

Of course, I have to say that being willing to get to the truth, it's a bit of a luxury. It's easier for some people to dig into it, because they can handle the consequences. I mean, if you are in a job situation where you have to work and you think that maybe your work is not the truth and what you're doing is not the truth but you have mouths to feed and you have limited opportunities, then you are going to be more reluctant – even if you have the intellectual capacity – to dig in. "I don't want to know that I shouldn't be doing this, that I should be doing something else, because that would create such crisis in my life, such a disturbance, that I would just let that one alone."

DAVID BLOOM: You were once in a situation where – for the sake of your soul – you felt you had to change careers. Tell me about it.

ANDREA COSNOWSKY: What lead me ultimately to become a rabbi was a moment of conscience. It wasn't until about nine months later that I actually made the decision. I was in Nashville. A friend of mine with whom I wrote was having this big showcase the next day. All of the A&R people were about to come, and everybody had RSVP'd. The day before this event was to take place, my friend overdosed on a bottle of sleeping pills and, I guess, vodka. I don't know. She took all these sleeping pills and called me. Of course, I didn't know what to do. I called 911 and raced to her house, but she lived far away and the ambulance got there first.

She lived, but we were in the hospital, and the tubes are coming out of her body, and I'm thinking how can we get her well enough so tomorrow she can do the showcase. I wasn't thinking I'm so sorry that my friend was in so much pain. I realized I don't want to be that person. I have become the cold, driven, shallow person that I never wanted to become. That, to me, was when I realized I wasn't living to my highest level. It wasn't about the people anymore. It was about my career and me, and that was no way to live.

By the time my friend overdosed, I hadn't been able to get back to really loving what I was doing. I did it for the sake of doing it, not because it was going to get me somewhere. I was very caught up in where my career was going and who I could call and who I could angle to get in. I had lost that beauty which I had gotten into songwriting for in the first place. That's when I decided to become a rabbi.

Character cannot be developed in ease and quiet. Only through experience of trial and suffering can the soul be strengthened, ambition inspired, and success achieved.

-Helen Keller

BARRETT DOSS: Soul is something that you have to develop on your own. I think somebody else can give you inspiration and can inspire you to put more into it. If someone really loves something, they can inspire you.

DAVID BLOOM: Do you feel that your soulfulness has changed at all over the past five or six years?

BARRETT DOSS: I don't think my soulfulness has changed in the last five or six years. I don't think I had it before I realized what I really loved and what I really wanted to do. I was swimming and I liked it, but I didn't really, really love it. I was singing, but I wasn't singing really seriously. I didn't know what I loved, so I don't think I had it yet. I developed it over time when I began to sing more and began to learn how to do different things with my voice and discovered musical theater and jazz and music in general. When I started to do more of it, I think that's when I really got soul.

BILL HORBERG: I've looked at my life as a perpetual search for soul. I have always been drawn to the arts, to storytelling, to musical idioms. For me, what's been compelling is my curiosity about discovering the authenticity that's available out there in the human experience. Seeking out and finding those moments where we are connected deeply with our roots, with some interior world that we need to express and communicate – with some vision of our place in the universe.

I think everybody has a soul. The way people are in touch with their soul – the way that they feel comfortable manifesting their soulfulness in exchange with other people – is very much determined and shaped by their upbringing and their life experience. A search for something that's real and has within it something that touches us, that thrills us, that tickles us – all of those things go beyond the kind of plastic veneer and get into our guts. What we so desperately want is a return to a human scale of what we're fully involved in.

DAVID BLOOM: Has having a child influenced your values and ultimately, your soul?

ELSA MORA: Having my first baby, that was a big change for me, because before I had her, I was very focused on my work, my art. It was all about that. All about enjoying that little place where I used to be most of the time, but then she took me out of there. Like, "Wait, life is not only about you. You have to think about me too." It was very demanding every night breastfeeding her. Not sleeping enough. Those were hard feelings physically and emotionally. I had to learn a new way to be as a person, to give more, to be less selfish, because even when you enjoy what you do and you do it with a big passion, that doesn't mean that you are perfect – because you created the whole world.

You also have to be selfish; you can get lost into that little world that you create. I had to learn everything has a limit, and I have to work, because I need to do it. I just have to do it, but I have to have a limit. Okay, I'm going to stop at 5:00 PM. Then after that time, I'm going to forget about myself, and I'm going to try to give my family the best I can. In that way, I do think that having a family changes a lot of what I am. I feel like I'm a better person. I understand many things better, things that I didn't think about before, about children. I remember some time when my mom was ignoring me and how hurt I felt, so I don't want that to happen to me. That's why you grow up in some way. You become better, because you become more responsible. That's what I felt. It happened to me.

DAVID BLOOM: Can people find soul at any age?

STUDS TERKEL: Dave Dellinger, who was a conscientious objector during World War Two, was one of the Chicago Conspiracy Eight on trial [in 1968, for demonstrating against the Vietnam War]. Now Dave's father was a very, very conservative lawyer who was ashamed of his son, and he felt disgraced by his son who had served time in prison for being a CO.

Dave knew one thing about his father: He was very conservative, but on a certain occasion when the family went out to eat to celebrate the mother's birthday – and the father's dressed up and the mother is in a nice gown – the waiter or waitress got nervous and spilled soup on the mother's dress. The father says, "Oh, oh, no! It's my fault, it's my fault! I tipped your hand." Dave said, "I knew my father wasn't within ten feet of her. He always had respect for the person serving him. He took the blame himself. He was really a man of a good soul, see."

So when the father was dying, he said to Dave toward the end, "Maybe, Dave, you were right about the Vietnam War." And his father was changing. "Maybe you, my son, were right after all, and you did the human thing to do." And Dave said, "Dad, I learned that from you." Now that's a great story, because it goes beyond politics. He could be this right-wing guy and also a decent soul.

Re-examine all that you have been told...
dismiss that which insults your soul.

-Walt Whitman

CHRISTIAN STEINBARTH: Soul is kind of like muscles or things like that. If you use it enough, you can develop it so it's always there. It's kind of like a habit. To make yourself soulful, I think maybe you use your personality or some trait that will just make you happy every time you use it. For some people, they really think that gift-giving makes them feel good, which is great. Because when they do that, that's how they're being soulful. You might not feel very strongly about something, but a single action, a single event could just set you off, make you feel energetic about an idea.

DAVID BLOOM: Are you saying that any soulful behavior could spontaneously emerge, even though it might not be the way you normally act?

ANN SAWYER: I don't think it necessarily has to be something you say or something materialized. It can just be something you think, like you're just thinking about something good and telling someone. Maybe if I make them feel good, maybe that will make me feel good. Soulfulness can be spurred pretty spontaneously. If there is something really bad that happens and you find that you are able to just come through, if you lose someone really close to you and you are able to keep on going, I think that your soul might grow.

NATHAN WORCESTER: A lot of people think that it is better to give than to receive. For humanitarians that is really true. But I am sure that by giving, they are really receiving some very… I guess you could call it karma or something like that. But seeing a place horrible enough that it needs to have humanitarian aid will really change someone – and probably change their soul too.

BARRETT DOSS: If somebody does a good deed going to somewhere like a deprived country or something, they shouldn't do it because they think, "That will be good for my soul." It should be more that that's what they really want to do.

CHRISSY DELACOTTA: I think some people think of soul as a scoreboard where it's like, "Hey, I helped Old Man Jenkins cross the street today. That's one more point for my soul." It's something that you have to keep. A terrible example – but I think it's a good example – is playing guitar. If you play a guitar for a while and then you stop, if you didn't really concentrate on it, it's going to go away and you're going to lose it. But if you slowly keep doing it for a long period of time, it will stay at that same level and you'll have it forever. I think that's what a soul does.

JON SWANK: So in other words, there is a certain element of soul in sincerity. You might do something that's good because, on the soul scoreboard, you're hedging your bets as to whether there's an afterlife or not. You want to make sure you go to a good place. But there's a certain amount of sincerity that's demanded to be soulful. Sometimes someone who is either soulless or clueless behaves like that and they discover – with the connection with people – that they improve their soul. They make themselves grow.

BARRETT DOSS: Everybody can develop soul. I don't think it's something you're born with. Well, maybe. You might be born with the need for soul inside you, but I don't think it shows in everybody. I don't think everyone can discover it for themselves. They should be able to, but some people either don't have the drive or need, and others might not care. That's why not everybody has it, because some people might not want it. Some people might not think they need it, but everyone is capable of having soul. I don't think everyone can find it.

Some bad things have happened to me in my life. There was a period where I didn't really have any friends in school (because of a mean girl). I didn't have anybody to talk to except for my mom and my family. Slowly after that, I started realizing I need to get back on the horse and keep moving. I can't stop. I'm too social a person. I'm too friendly a person to cut myself off from the rest of the world for my entire life. I slowly started talking to people who either knew about what happened but didn't let me know that they knew, or that didn't know at all. I started talking to them, and I gradually got back into the swing of things. I still haven't really talked to this girl for, I guess, three or four years now, but I definitely think that helped me learn about soul, because I knew that there was something inside of me that wasn't right for a while.

ZACK GRAHAM: Part of finding your soul is just stripping down everything that is unimportant and finding the side that really makes you, you. If you know yourself and the truth, you can use that to make unimaginable things happen.

NATALIJA NOGULICH: Soul is an effortless thing. It is a part of our being. It IS our being. But what happens is, we wreck it and inhibit it and tear it down – or the world does or society or our parents, or something out there, is going to try and take a swing at us. But we have it, you know.

We've just got to keep it clear, keep the passage clear, keep the trash out so it can radiate forth. And that can be a full-time job.

CLIFF COLNOT: If someone were to ask me, "Do you consider yourself soulful?" I would say I aspire to be soulful. I am clearly aware of what values and behaviors I need to hold and exhibit to be soulful, and I aspire to be consistent in those behaviors and values. For me personally, the evolution of the soulfulness quotient in my own life has been gradual. There have been no epiphanies, no moments of dramatic insight vis-à-vis soulfulness. It's been a work in progress that has had a certain ebb and flow but largely has been gradual over many years. I don't always succeed, but it has been and continues to be a personal goal of mine to be soulful.

DAVID BLOOM: Can you tell me about somebody who changed their soul dramatically?

STUDS TERKEL: Yes, the former Grand Cyclops of the Ku Klux Klan, C.P. Ellis. He of all people led me to feel that anybody can change, depending on circumstance and fortune or whatever may be the case. It wasn't a metamorphosis; it was just a gradual series of epiphanies, you might say, a gradual series of discoveries of how he was being used by the big boys. He was poor and all of his life was miserable. He felt that he failed – and who's to blame? Well, he'd been taught all of his life: "the nigger," that's what the guys told him. So he joins the Klan.

Now it's the 1960s, the civil rights movement's just beginning, and there was a certain woman in his town, a black woman, name was Ann Atwater. They would hate each other with such rage, and he used to break up her picket lines, these picket lines trying to persuade, force the department stores of Durham, North Carolina, to hire black clerks. Then one day things happen, and these two find themselves in the same boat: She has a girl going to school, he has a boy going to school, and they realize they're both being used. From then on, through knowing her and working with her and the experiences that they shared, he became a spokesman for civil rights and civil liberties, and he found himself as a person.

It was also going to visit her church and hearing some of that music that he found familiar. He's a white churchgoer, but some of the hymns are similar, like "Beulah Land." "Beulah Land" is both a black and a white song – "Oh, Beulahland," and as they were swinging, he was tapping his foot. And she said to me, "I knew I had him going then." You might say his soul was touched.

DAVID BLOOM: All forms of artistic expression can touch the soul, whatever they are.

RICK KOGAN: Look at a building! You don't have to know anything about architecture to say, "That is a beautiful building." You don't have to know anything about painting to appreciate a painting. But life puts these pressures on so you can't say to one of your banking colleagues, "I really like that painting," because they will then say, "Well, why do you say that?" And you think – because of movies and everything you've ever heard – that you're supposed to say, "Well, it's representative of a movement from the X movement school…" Nonsense!

Don't be ashamed to say you like something! Don't be ashamed to experience something! It can't hurt you! That's part of the secret language of soul: the ability to allow yourself to respond to the amazing and infinite number of wonders that life presents to you every day. Nobody has time to do it all, but allow yourself to experience wonder, and you will touch whatever it is that's your soul.

ERWIN DRECHSLER: All too often we think it's about us. But the big picture is a lot bigger than we think it is or know it is. We're just a little part in it for a short period of time, so be focused. Care about one another. Care about yourself – and care about what you eat.

We had people in this restaurant that come in a bad mood. Some things happened to them. They've had a crappy day. They've had an argument. By the time they leave and we say goodbye to them, they're different people. Something has happened. We like to think that we're a part of that shift in terms of changing their mood.

DAVID BLOOM: So it's a culinary divine intervention.

ERWIN DRECHSLER: With some people – if they allow it to happen, yes.

DAVID BLOOM: Where else can you find divine interventions?

ELSA MORA: I grew up with my mom always directing the right way, telling you the right things. I think that's the beginning of how you start having a soul in your life, when things come more from somebody else. But there is a time in your life where things are coming out from yourself, so that's when soul starts happening to you. It's something different, something that makes me very comfortable when I think about developing my spirituality.

You know what? I have a little universe inside me. I don't want to abandon that. The opposite, I want to go there and stay there as much as possible, and that's what I've been doing for years. That's why I say that soul is a place you build for yourself, and you can invite people to come into that place and enjoy it with you. That's what makes life special sometimes – and really worthwhile.

BOB WILLEMS: Soul is a work in progress, it's an endeavor. In fact, one of the highest forms of human endeavor is to pursue your soul as an individual. Soul is unique to you, it's unique to me, it's unique to everybody in the world – but it's connected in a more broad way. The analogy that I think of is it's like water. You can take a drop of water and it's water. It stands on its own. It's H_2O. Put it in a glass, mix it with some ice and have it to drink. But you can throw it in the ocean and it becomes a part of the ocean, and it's water for the rest of the world. I think the soul is a similar thing.

There's a unique spirit in each individual, and there's something only they can do. It's not something that someone else can tell you how to find, or give you a book on "Fifty different ways to find your soul and apply it to your career." It's something you have to search for by yourself. Part of that process is grappling with what is the soul. What is it that you're searching for? One of the big hurdles in society today is people don't ask these kind of questions. They're distracted. All these commercial activities: How do I make money, what do I need to buy next? The real questions are way more fundamental than that.

It's impossible to think about how are you going to find your unique spirit, the thing that drives your person in the deepest kind of way, without even thinking about "What am I, who am I as an individual? What are those questions I have to ask myself to figure out what is my identity about and what is my life going to be about?" I think that without establishing your identity and really doing something in a deliberate way, it's impossible to pursue any soulful activities.

DAVID BLOOM: You see a tremendous variety of patients. Are they – for lack of a better description – on a journey to their soul?

CHARLES JAFFE: People come here because they feel in some way lost. Their best efforts to express themselves, their best efforts to adapt in the world, are not going well. If they were going well, they wouldn't be here. In fact, it's a necessary quality to accept that being in this room is to be an active participant in a search. It's not passive at all.

There are all kinds of people, so there are all kinds of being lost, all kinds of journeys. Sometimes it's jaw-dropping amazing to see the range of things that people can produce in their imagination or from their defenses or in their relationships with people. The kinds of journeys: They range from getting through every day without killing themselves, to searching for forms of creative expression, to being able to maintain a sense of individuality in the face of relationships, to being parents.

For people who come to this office, we have to do a lot of work to turn their eyes inward and seek their own expression of their innermost self or soulfulness. They are all on a journey towards a richer articulation of their core, essential, human range of experience and expression.

NATALIJA NOGULICH: I think things could be turned around with the healing of individual consciousness. One, then two, then ten. Then a hundred. Then a thousand. Then on and on and on. It has to start with an individual consciousness that says, "No, I will not hate. I'm going to choose not to hate." That doesn't mean that we live in lawlessness. That doesn't mean that we tolerate crime. It means that we punish the crime, but we don't hate the ignorance that caused the crime. We try to educate it. And one person has to start somewhere to stop the cycle of hate. It can't be legislated; we've proved that, haven't we?

The politics are going to continue, and also religious intolerance and things that make Saddam Hussein gas two hundred thousand people. For what? Because they called their belief a different word from what I call mine? That has to be arrested. I'm not interested in tolerating that. But I am interested in looking in my consciousness for a way to love a little bit better today because I believe that the individual consciousness can affect and ripple out to change the world.

What if every damn body on this planet just prayed for ten minutes a day to love better? I know it sounds kind of Pollyanna, but I think it would make a difference. I really, sincerely do. Instead of my thinking you're a little different from me, I don't want you around, I say, "But you know, there's a lot about us that is the same. There's one thing that's the same. Let me look at that."

DAVID BLOOM: Does healing your conscience constitute a form of rebirth? As a rabbi, a religious leader, would you say you've been born again?

ANDREA COSNOWSKY: On some level, yes, I've been born again. But more than using such a loaded term, I'd say that I've worked very hard to be rid of what blocks me from the sunlight of the spirit, from God and from other people. The more ego I have, the less room there is for soul. The more it's not about me, the bigger my soul can be. The more room it has to touch others.

DAVID BLOOM: Have you met people who you felt had some kind of awakening, enlightenment, epiphany – in terms of their soulfulness?

BOB WILLEMS: Yes. For a part of my career, I was doing recruiting for an environmental advocacy organization. My role was to go to these college recruitment offices where I was sitting next to the guy from Leo Burnett Advertising and the guy from a consulting firm who was going to pay ten times what we were going to pay. My mission was to go and find those students who were open to the idea of doing something that was not about commercial success or not about building status in their lives, and to present to them the idea that "You've educated yourself, you've built these tools in your life to accomplish something. Is there something other than financial success that you can accomplish with those things?"

Throughout the recruitment season, I would talk to hundreds of college graduates who had just got done from their interview with the bank down the hall. You could tell that the interviews they went through had roughly the same format: "What are your skills, what do you like to do, what don't you like to do?" And then they'd come in to my interview, and I'd say, "What do you want to change about the world?" or "What would you do to fix the problems that you see in the world?" And to them it was like, you can almost see it happen in front of your eyes. That's not the question they were told they were going to be asked in the interview. They were not prepared for the answer.

I don't think the interviews themselves actually changed anybody, but the people who were seriously considering this as a choice, at least for a short term in their careers, they go through the interviews, they investigate it, or they're open to the idea that their life's going to be about something significant. These people, a year before that, might just be bereft of any kind of soulful stuff in their lives, but once you make that conscious decision – like "I'm acting deliberately and I've thought for myself that the world has its pluses and minuses, but I see minuses that I want to do something about. That can be my work. That can be what I do for a job." – I think for many people that was the first step in their lives to actually pursue a deeper meaning and a more soulful approach to their lives. I hope it did.

I've kept in contact with a lot of people over the years, and they say it was my interview that changed their lives. It's like a little nudge in the trajectory of their life and they're on a different path; it can be that small of a change. I think these people had dramatic repercussions down the road.

ANDREA COSNOWSKY: There are people that listen to their soul and say, "I'm going to take this job even though it doesn't pay me as much money." They're so much happier because they are listening to what their soul is asking them to do. Or they're listening to what their soul is asking them to be. I believe that is our objective as humans, as spiritual beings. Having a spiritual experience is to get in touch with that voice, to that part of our soul, because it will never lead us in the wrong direction if we're only willing to listen to it.

DON MEADE: We've got to get back to the human element and start dealing with people again. And maybe we'll find ourselves. Maybe. I don't think I'll see it in my lifetime. Now, I'm willingly sticking my neck out because I don't know how long I'm going to live. There's a little bit too much sorting out to do, and I'm not sure I trust who's going to sort it out.

We can't get away from the fact that we all have this soul. Now what we do with it, that's another thing. They say that we only use, what? half of our intelligence – or even less. That depends on what you want, what you're in pursuit of. You know, happiness has a strange meaning. To a dog, happiness is a good soup bone. It's all there. We have to pursue it, we have to search for it. But we misinterpret a lot of things. The Constitution is a good example of that. It said you have the right to pursue; it didn't say you're going to find it. It said you have the right to go out and beat the bushes. Maybe it's there, maybe it's not. You are allowed that right. Deny that right and you might not ever know what was in the bushes. If anything was there at all!

We tell kids in our society, "You're as good as any, go out there and give it your best shot." Your best shot oftentimes isn't good enough. No, no, they have to go back and be tutored and nurtured by someone who's been there already. We don't seek to do that in the Western world. We don't take advice from someone who's been there. Okay, someone that's been there, that was their time, and we create these divisions and say, "That was his time, this is now." Nothing changes; it's just soup warmed over again. The more things change, the more they stay the same. This is history.

DAVID BLOOM: Is it ever too late to reawaken your soul?

BOB WILLEMS: My dad passed away when I was a senior in high school. He had a stroke which basically left him paralyzed on one side of his body and affected his thinking in a pretty significant way. He was a very changed man. But in a very, very significant way there was very little change about him. His thinking wasn't quite as clear. He wasn't able to use parts of his body. He was in the hospital for most of the last year of his life. But the core of his person was vibrant; he was still there.

It was like he was going through these huge, painful medical procedures and still very open and joking around. The spirit of the person… People fear health problems like that all their lives. They think, "How can I prevent that more than anything else?" In fact, it changed what his experience of his life was like. But did it change him as a person? No, not at all. Not even a little bit.

DAVID BLOOM: As a physician, you often face the death of a patient. How does that affect your soul?

CHARLES JAFFE: When I was a freshmen medical student, I did some volunteer work in the emergency room. I remember the first time I walked in, I was paralyzed with fear that if I breathed or touched anyone or touched anything, I would kill somebody. Everything in the emergency room is all about life and death. A wise old sophomore medical student turned to me and said, "Just remember. Nothing matters." It was so paradoxical to the way I was feeling at that moment – and it so alerted me to how terrified I was – that it became a kind of mantra for me.

DAVID BLOOM: He didn't mean it in a nihilistic way?

CHARLES JAFFE: Not a bit. It was a paradoxical intervention that he really picked up, instantly, how frightened I was, and he responded in a kind of exaggerated, humorous, ironic, sarcastic way that was brilliantly placed for me. Somebody else could have heard it in a very, very different way, but to me it opened the door.

I think it's a kind of perspective that's grown in me and has allowed me to not be so afraid of looking all around my innards, if you will. It's not something I talk about with patients, but when I'm referencing an ideal for human connectedness and the humility of people in relation to one another, it's definitely had an influence on my development.

I'm kind of an anxious person, and that touchstone of "Just remember, nothing matters" and the irony about that has become woven into my personality. I still often get anxious in new situations, and then I hear myself saying, "Just remember, nothing matters."

HOLDING ON TO YOUR SOUL

Old Brazilian man — Felipe Frazeo

The principal thing in the world is the keep the soul afloat.

-Erica Jong

Only a man who knows what it is like to be defeated can reach down to the bottom of his soul and come up with the extra ounce of power it takes to win when the match is even.

-Muhammad Ali

    The pursuit of soulfulness – for an individual, a community, or a nation – never ends. Once attained, soul requires upkeep; otherwise, it risks deterioration, even loss. But great effort brings great rewards: self-knowledge, joy, wonder, and the ability to give and receive love.

    Participants in this chapter suggest a few techniques to maintain soulfulness; clearly, many other methods can – and will – come to mind. You are invited to explore more about soul by visiting *www.whatissoul.com*.

ELSA MORA: Soul is something you feel a little bit every day. It's impossible to touch, to see, but you know it's there. It's even something that can save your life.

DAVID BLOOM: Where do people find the inner resources to remain soulful?

TOM BURRELL: I think solitude is a part and parcel of finding soul. Some people have an easier time in finding it than others. Some people need to spend less time in solitude, but it certainly is necessary to be quiet and to get in touch with yourself.

RICK KOGAN: The inability to be by oneself is one of the biggest impediments to achieving soul. I know people who can't stand to be alone, and those people who are alone can't stand to be quiet. They've got to have something on, they've got to have something going, they've got to have television, they've got to have radio. But just to sit and think, it doesn't happen.

One of the most joyful parts of life is to be still. That's the way I spent my New Year's, and that's the way I plan to spend them as long as I can, just sitting and thinking and reflecting. It's great. It's a terrific joy to be in touch with yourself.

CHARLES JAFFE: The role of being alone – in one's development over a lifespan – is very different for different people. For some, being alone can be a deeply opening, flowering experience. At the other end of the spectrum, there are people who need the company of others – or an engagement with something – as a vehicle for expression of their deepest self. It really depends.

There's a sequence that small children go through where they actually develop the capacity to be alone. First they can't be alone at all, and then they learn to be alone in the company of someone else. Eventually, they learn to be alone on their own, in a satisfying way. An essential quality about being human is all wrapped up in that dynamic. Being in relation or being on one's own – and that emotional experience – is what captures someone's essence, expresses their innermost self: their soulfulness.

BILL KURTIS: Well, you have to know who you are, and you have to come to it. For me, I enjoyed what I was doing. I enjoyed reporting, seeing the world around me, telling that story. And so I was so busy doing that, that I really didn't think a lot about everything else. But when you start to write books or make decisions that require you to know who you are, you require solitude. That doesn't mean two hundred fifty e-mails that take you two hours to go through every morning when you come to work. That is another barrier that we have put up with. It's almost a barrier to communication – rather than improving it.

I find a lot of people are going to the wide open spaces to find a little plot of land where they can look at the sunset and just kind of be. Rather than looking at the watch, meeting that next appointment, you get into a rhythm of the Earth and seasons that become the time that you really value.

ANN SAWYER: Soul should be a thing of joy and not a thing of burden at all. It should just be great.

BARRETT DOSS: When people say they can see it in your eyes that you enjoy doing something, that's where soul is. I think when someone can see it looking in from the outside, that's when you know you have soul. Someone else can see it. You're emoting it. Soul is involved in anything that you really love.

STUDS TERKEL: Love and soul are intertwined. And the love – here I sound like a preacher – it's not a question of loving a person in a romantic way. I'd equate love with respect. Or there's a romantic love and there's love of a friend. But to a great extent to me, it's respect for the Other, who may disagree with you.

Love makes your soul crawl out from its hiding place.

-Zora Neale Hurston

TOM BURRELL: Soul and true love start with you delving into yourself to determine what's important to you and what love really is, and then what and who you love. When we start talking about what love has to do with soul, I think we need to define what love is. My rough definition of love: unconditional, unselfish, good wishes for another person or thing. When you love something or you love someone, you want the best for that thing or that one. What most people really mean when they say "I love you" is "I love the way that you make me feel," which is different, because those two things actually lead to totally different kinds of behaviors and reactions.

When you love someone, you are thinking about that person. When you love the way somebody makes you feel, you are thinking about your condition. So the idea of "I love you and I want to be with you all the time," it's not a fit. Especially if the person who is being loved wants to be left alone. It's like, "If you love me, leave me alone, don't bother me."

BILL HORBERG: Soul is love and love is soul. When you're able to love and be loved, you've found the ability to open up a window on your soul, to listen and hear the music of another person. I think that's the journey that we're all on.

BOB WILLEMS: In some ways, the most complicated thing in the world is to just make your life about love. In other ways, it's the most simple thing you could possibly do. Just strip everything else out there. All these priorities. Just love. Love everybody in the world. Love your neighbor like yourself. How can you not have long-term life lessons out of that?

BARRETT DOSS: Love is something that really drives me. Whether it's love for my family, love for music, love for art. In my experience that is what helped me get through a lot of the hard times, the bad things that happened to me in my life. That helped me move on, and that helped me find my soul. That's why I connect love and soul so much, because for me they were so closely knit in my experience. Without love you can have soul, but without soul you can't really have love.

DAVID BLOOM: Did you learn anything about love and soul from your parents?

BILL KURTIS: I can't think of a specific involving my parents. With my father it was more an example of quiet strength. Someone who is always there. And the most wonderful thing was being able to call home and know that they're always going to be at the other end of the line with a kind word. That is kind of a foundation that allowed me to fly around the world, almost like an astronaut in space, tethered back to love, unconditional love.

DAVID BLOOM: One of my favorite quotes of Abraham Heschel is "That which we can't comprehend by analysis, we become aware of in awe." Sometimes awe makes us go "Wow!" At other times it makes us feel wonder. Is there a difference between wow and wonder?

RICK KOGAN: Wow is a nifty Michael Jordan move. Wonder is a blade of grass. I really believe that. Wow is a high five; wonder is a kiss with someone you love. Wow is making thirty-eight thousand dollars in two minutes at the Commodities Exchange, and wonder is a bus driver who says, "Hi, good morning. How are you today?" There are a million examples. I appreciate a Michael Jordan great move to the bucket when I say "Wow." But you stare at a piece of grass: "How did this happen?" Or stare at a cloud! You know, wow is fireworks – and I like fireworks! Wonder is clouds.

I'm not going to say that, at my advanced age, being awed is better than an orgasm, but it's up there. I think life is so special and precious, that people deserve to be awed. Open your eyes to the wonder around you! If you cannot find something wonderful – I don't care where you live, I don't care what your life is like – if you cannot find something, one thing wonderful every day, you're wasting your life and you are abusing whatever your soul might be. It's all just a matter of keeping your eyes open. Just open your eyes!

I begin every single day by standing in the middle of the Michigan Avenue bridge, and I do a complete three hundred sixty degree turn, slowly, to look at the majesty of those buildings, most of them built by big corporations. Then you have the natural flow (or unnatural, because they reversed the natural flow) of the river. It's the most beautiful spot on Earth. You feel small (I do, when I stand there), which allows me some perspective through the day so that if the smallest nice thing happens to me, I cherish it.

I'll look at each of these buildings and think Jesus, how many thousands of people are working there? I wish I could have been there, watching the guys who put the girders up. I look around at the buildings and think, "Did someone design that building? I wonder who that was." I wonder what sort of strange, inspired lunatic said, "I'm going to build for the Wrigley family something that looks like a birthday cake!"

I feel awed and inspired at the same time. It was people who built this city, from a black man trading fur, to soldiers fighting off the Indians. And here we are. Here?! You see what I mean? It's a weird way of feeling connected to the present, but also, for me, to the past.

DAVID BLOOM: I find it sad when people are unable to feel awe, having lost that ability at some point in their lives.

RICK KOGAN: People don't let themselves see it! I think it is as possible to be awed by a ladybug as it is by a tiger. If you allowed yourself, and you had time and let yourself go, the sunrise over Lake Michigan should awe you every morning. There is no doubt about it. I've told people who really feel depressed, "Hey, you know what? Go out tonight and have four cocktails – or five, depending on how big you are – have four or five cocktails, try to get a good night's sleep. Go out tomorrow morning, wherever you live, go down to the lake – and watch the sunrise. You are going to feel better." Because awe gives you a sense, not only of place, but of wonder. If you let yourself think about it, there is wonder in a tiger. There is wonder in a flower. There is wonder in a tree. There is wonder even in Formica! There is wonder all over this world. Allow yourself to trip over it. It's everywhere! There is wonder in another person – what they feel, what they think, how they look, what they do and why they do it. Life can be a remarkable experience if you just stay open to it. I do not think that this is some random nonsense that you're you and I'm me. There's a purpose here, man!

AFTERWORD

Congratulations on finishing the book. I hope it has been as engaging and valuable to you as it has been to me.

During the last fifteen years of interviewing people about soul, I have had an education on the range and contexts where soul exists. Many of my interviewees use the word "soul" in an elevated, virtuous way, just as I had before listening to psychiatrist Charles Jaffe. He said soul can be pretty stinky at times, defining it as all that is human: the attitudes, behaviors, emotions and stories that people tell. Not just the good stuff.

Although I agree with Jaffe concerning the word soul, I believe 'soulful' means what I initially felt, that it describes people filled with a deep passion for who they are, what they do and how they empathize with other people. Soulful people want to share their unique gifts with others. They want to touch other souls. They differentiate themselves from others by the strength of their output of soul.

To see, hear, or feel soul, it is critical to be receptive to it. Otherwise, it can go right through you – or over or beneath you – but unfortunately not hit you. It's clear to me that brilliant musical performances come from and can move the soul. But I have learned that soul can be found in unsuspected places.

Soul is not necessarily loud or soft, bright or subdued, large or small. It is not fast or slow. The speed of soul is as variable as the full range of human emotion and behavior. When we experience soul from another person, we experience their true nature. Soul is what is real in people.

The gathering of all the soulful experiences we have had informs and strengthens our souls as we travel through life. Going through the motions, and behaving as others want us to, is anything but soulful. It is only through a sincere appreciation of our uniqueness, and what we can bring to the world, that we discover our fundamental soulfulness.

I genuinely hope that this book has dramatically enhanced your appreciation of soul, in yourself and others, and that it will stimulate you to look at other people as sources of soul. Each time we have a soul encounter, it encourages us to live soulfully, which is real living.

-David Bloom

Acknowledgements

I would like to thank all of the interviewees for their involvement in **What Is Soul?** Their efforts have created a tapestry of thoughts, feelings and experiences for us to use as we further our inquiries about soul.

This book would not have been completed without a supportive, energetic and skilled staff. Barbara Kaplan has been the linchpin in the completion of the book. Her input has been critical in each phase: reading all interviews, determining what should be included and not, organizing the chapters, and finally a hard edit of the text. Hannah Frank has been very helpful clarifying parts of the book. Reynaldo Certain has designed a very handsome looking layout for all to see and appreciate.

Also, a group of people I call my brain trust, the people who have had various levels of impact on the book, have all had an encouraging and uplifting effect on me in general. They include: Jon Marable, Paula Hoffman, Cliff Colnot, Janet Landay, Susan Kimmel, Ben Counts, Tom Burrell, Jeff Pinzino, Victoria Martin and Neal Peterson.

For more information please visit
www.WhatIsSoul.com

www.ingramcontent.com/pod-product-compliance
Lightning Source LLC
Chambersburg PA
CBHW060511300426
44112CB00017B/2621